Indoor decorative plants and cut flowers

INDOOR DECORATIVE PLANTS and cut flowers

Leslie Johns

WARD LOCK & CO. LIMITED
LONDON AND SYDNEY

7063 1125 6

Printed in Great Britain by William Clowes and Sons, Limited,
London and Beccles

CONTENTS

Scindapsus
A good screen and climbing plant

1 DECORATING THE HOME WITH PLANTS AND FLOWERS

Flowers and plants are essential to all human life. Apart from the fact that from some of them we obtain our food and without these we could not constantly replenish our flesh, muscles and stores of nervous energy, there is a deeper need within us all for some basic contact with nature that can sometimes only be provided by placing flowers and plants among our otherwise lifeless, sterile and over-functional surroundings. And from flowers and plants we get a deep, sensual pleasure that helps to distinguish us, the human race, from all other animals.

To most of us, however, the practicalities of decorating our homes with flowers and plants are of greater importance than the philosophic background to our needs and our pleasures, and here we are fortunate in having available so wide a choice of plant material that we can indulge our tastes, flatter our furnishings and experiment with colours, textures, shapes and forms.

A long lasting arrangement of chrysanthemums

Decorating the home with plants and flowers

Plants and flowers in the home are basically furnishings. They soften the scene, give intimacy and personality to what can otherwise be a somewhat bleak and severe background. And although cut flowers in containers have a somewhat limited life, with reasonable care many pot plants will live, grow and fulfil their decorative function for many months, so proving to be highly economical in use. It is, in fact, the sheer economy of flowers and plants as furnishings that gives us a guide to their treatment, for all styles of arrangement with both cut flowers and living plants are primarily means of so using, so placing them that we show them to greatest advantage. The banded bunch of daffodils from the florist can be placed as it is in a jug of water, but this way several of the flowers will be hidden from view. Arranged, each flower shows and gives value.

So if we regard our potted plants and our cut flowers as an economical means of furnishing the home, we understand that they have a purposeful as well as a decorative role to play. The bright bowl of flowers in the entrance hall, for example, serves to lighten what is frequently a comparatively dark area, it serves to set the scene of warmth and humanity inside the home and it is both a welcome and a compliment to the arriving guest. Flowers and plants should be consciously employed to fulfil a function.

The vivid colours of anemones help to give warmth in the cold days of winter, while cool greens and whites help to soften the harsh outer heat of the summer sun. Green plants for some reason appear both to cool the atmosphere in summer and warm it in winter, levelling out the seasons and promoting comfort regardless of weather.

But although seasons dictate the availability of some flowers and plants, many are available the whole year through and can be used to still more conscious purpose. Flowers and plants always draw attention to themselves, which suggests that they can be employed to conceal, disguise or draw the eyes away from a shabby piece of furniture or an uninspiring view from a window. Equally they can highlight a picture on the wall, serve as a link between the colours of curtains and carpet, accent the graceful line of a chair, give height to a low

Monstera deliciosa
(Swiss cheese plant)

room, lengthen a short one, provide a talking point and fill many other functions as well as the more obvious one of providing simple decoration.

In very general terms it is possible to differentiate between flowers and plants for home decoration largely because flowers usually have greater colour impact and a briefer life and plants have greater form, a more sculptural effect. Even where we use flowering plants and so get the best of both worlds, these seldom have the long life in perfect condition as enjoyed by foliage plants, and we must bear in mind the fact that in all decoration with flowers and plants these must always appear fresh, well groomed, crisp and alive. Nothing gives a shabby look to a room so much as tired, wilting, diseased or thirsty flowers and plants.

Although flowers will continue to grow and develop even after they have been cut from their parent plants, so long as they are carefully conditioned and placed in water, they will not grow to the same extent as some foliage plants. For some of these, notably *Rhoicissus rhomboidea, Cissus antarctica,* ivies and the Swiss cheese plant, *Monstera deliciosa*, will grow to cover an entire

A flat-backed arrangement of flowers

A striking bonsai wisteria. Some of these miniature trees have been known to live for hundreds of years

wall with suitable support. This is a valuable attribute of which we can well take advantage when required, but it should not be forgotten that many foliage plants can really grow too large for their surroundings after a few years of careful attention, and this fact should be carried in the mind when selecting plants, for this habit of growth can be an embarrassment as well as an advantage. Careful pruning and training to shape can assist in achieving the pattern and size demanded by the physical surroundings, and over-rampant growth can be slowed by the withholding of fertilizers or the confinement of the plant to an over-small pot, but in the long run if this is the habit of the plant too much discipline will lead only to its eventual disfigurement and death.

Today one large room is often made to contain the functions of several, being dining room and kitchen, or hall and living room, possibly with a kitchen annexe. Formal and restricting separations are not required, yet some indication of a division of function appears to be preferable. Plants can fulfil this requirement admirably, particularly those that climb and twine and form a natural screen or hedge. These curtaining plants must

Ficus elastica
(Rubber plant)
At the foot is
a trailing ivy

necessarily be large enough to do their job, but need not be alone. They can be complemented by others which will operate a decorative rather than screening purpose; plants of special value for their colour or their shape, plants which can if required be replaced when past their best with others of the same kind or by refreshing strangers.

Yet somehow, possibly through changes in personal taste, perhaps because of the times in which we live, as a result of the architectural style of our homes or the cleaner lines of our furnishings, somehow few if any of us can revert to the styles of a hundred years ago, when plant decorations were massed solidly against one wall, a herbaceous border of banked colour, tier upon tier of greenhouse or conservatory plants lined up regimentally to slay the neighbours and impress the casual visitor. Today each single plant must play a purpose, every flower arrangement is designed with an end in view. For our tastes have become more sophisticated and our talents more diversified. Quantity has been supplanted by quality and a cool, quiet appraisal of function has replaced a desire to stupefy by masses of vulgar and ostentatious colour.

Simultaneously, one should realise, accept and make use of the sculptural shape of so many foliage plants. The well-known rubber plant, *Ficus elastica*, the Swiss cheese plant, *Monstera deliciosa*, the palmate leaves and erect shape of *Fatshedera lizei* and several others are ideal against the clean lines of modern decor and furniture. Either standing against a wall or in the centre of a room these plants have a dignity and importance that makes it well worth while to have them as residents. They demand little attention, require no support other than a possible central stake and will live for years with modest care.

More training is required by some of the climbers and scramblers, for their habit is by nature less restrained and disciplined, but they can do a wonderful decorative job in the home, climbing a central cane, trained to grow up a wall or left to scrabble downwards from a high container. Rhoicissus, cissus, ivy, philodendrons, scindapsus and several others will cover a wall in a year or two. They again are easy, tolerant plants and so long as

This grouping of house plants can be used at the foot of a flight of stairs

a few minutes each week are devoted to training their exploratory tendrils they will go the way you wish and fulfil your desires in the way of screening, covering or disguising.

Little plant communities are a popular, distinctive and attractive way of creating a talking point in the home. Plants here can be widely varied, using some short and spreading, some tall and spiky, some green and some flowering, mixing them according to taste and talent, but being careful always to mix only those plants that have similar requirements. One would not, for example, put a water loving bog plant together with an arid cactus in the same container, for conditions necessary to the one would be deadly for the other.

These plant communities can be created in any kind of container large enough for them, from low, flat, square or rectangular troughs to Victorian footbaths or wash basins and even carboys. Nearly all plants enjoy living close to other plants, jostling each other and creating between themselves a little micro-climate of warmth and humidity. Feeding and tending is easier and quicker where all plants are grouped together and by using colour, texture and shape contrast it is possible to obtain striking and original effects.

The use of flowering plants in the home presents certain problems for most of us, for they can be employed only when they are in the peak of condition. Thus it is helpful to have a greenhouse to which they can be retired when they are past their best or from which they can be brought when approaching it. Lacking this a constant supply of flowering plants can be expensive, for they seldom last for more than a few weeks and tend to make somewhat greater demands on one's time in the way of picking off dead blooms, spraying, cleaning, grooming and otherwise ensuring that they appear at their best at all times.

Where a plant community has been created, however, it need be a matter of a few minutes only to remove the failing flowering plant and replace it with another from shop or greenhouse, thus giving the entire arrangement a brand new appearance. Where for practical reasons this is difficult, there is no cause why fresh cut flowers in a hidden, water-filled container should not be used instead of a flowering plant to give a vivid splash of colour, and in a later chapter I give suggestions on how this is best done.

But whether or not plants are grouped in communities it is always necessary indoors to stand potted plants in or on some kind of barrier between pot and furniture to prevent and avoid possible staining or damage. And if this is so there seems no reason why one should not take the final step and give each pot a permanent home in the form of an outer container larger than the plant pot itself. If the space between plant pot and outer container is filled with peat, sand, crumbled Florapak or Oasis or even crumpled newspaper, this will serve several purposes. In the first place this insulating layer will keep roots warm in winter and cool in summer. It will absorb any over-watering and release excess back to the roots when required. It will give off a minute quantity of humid air in the form of evaporation which will circulate up and around the foliage and thus benefit the plant. Finally

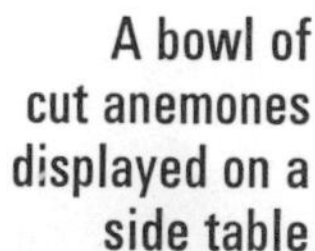

A bowl of cut anemones displayed on a side table

Trailing ivy
in an urn-
style container

Mixed arrangement
of hyacinths and
African violets

Arrangement of
house plants in
a pedestal-
style container

Corner of a sitting-room given over to foliage plants. All grow well away from direct light.

This arrangement of indoor plants is ideal for the end wall of a sitting-room or largish hall.

Mixed arrangement
of house plants
in a bowl

Mixed arrangement
of leaves and
fruits with an
orchid dominating

Mixed arrangement
of cut gladioli
and the leaves
of a begonia

Mixed arrangement of house plants in a pewter bowl

this container will, if correctly chosen, add to the decorative effect of the plant itself.

Where plants have largely an architectural or sculptural effect to play in indoor decoration, flowers with their greater and more vivid colour values have the more eye-catching appeal of a painting. Both have their functions.

Colours can be hot or cold, advancing or retiring, reflective or absorbing. All of these qualities can be used to obtain certain required effects. For example, if a room is long and narrow, dark and cold, it can be made to look shorter and wider, lighter and warmer by placing at the far end a glowing bowl of flowers, yellow, pink or white in hue. These colours are advancing, which means that the end of the room containing the flowers appears to come nearer, and if this happens the room will also appear to be wider. These colours are reflective, which means that they catch and reflect minimal quantities of available light. They are warm colours, which means that the room gives the impression of being warmer than it actually may be at the time.

All the foregoing exercises in the decorator's art become comparatively mechanical and automatic compared with the skill and taste demanded by the true home decorator, the arranger of flowers and plants according to colour blending, shape, form and texture, and this is the art that is captivating and enthralling women—and not a few men—all over the world.

Pittosporum, dieffenbachia and hedera and a sansevieria displayed in a fireplace

This is the exercise of using certain flowers or certain flowers and plants together because their contrast or blending of colour, shape, texture and form is more satisfying than the separate materials used alone. It is the art of selecting a flower or plant colour in all its tints and shades to form a link between, say, the cushion covers and the wallpaper. This is the skill of arranging plants or flowers into a formal or informal shape or pattern which blends, harmonises or contrasts with the line of a table, the curve of a chair back, the shape and texture of a fireplace. This is the impressing on flowers and plants by their choice and arrangement of style and personality, an expression of artistic talent as personal and unmistakable as a thumbprint.

Parenthetically, may I make it quite clear here at the beginning that to the flower arranger the word "flowers" is a generic term embracing all and any plant material living or dead. It includes, for example, all foliage, all fruits such as berries and even edible fruit, fungi, dried materials, grasses, even driftwood, twigs, branches and bark.

To the creative home decorator with flowers and plants this is the greatest art—and the greatest fun—of all. It is an art which can be learned by all, regardless of native talent, and one which, after the acquirement and understanding of certain basic techniques can suddenly blossom and lead to the creation of natural masterpieces of felicitous design. It is an art which all civilised men and women, town or country dwellers, can and should enjoy practising, for it is a part of living with nature, improving on nature and using nature to make the man-made world more endurable. It is an art which is both a kindliness and a compliment to fellow humans. It is an art which gives unexpected and delightful insights into the world around us: the true colours in brown, the complementary colour at the base of a tulip flower, the graceful lazy-S of a hanging ivy trail, the inexplicable and astonishing appearance of a cactus flower, the tender triumph in the training of a dwarf tree, the texture of an African violet leaf, the vivid but modest blush of a nidularium when it gives birth to its flowers.

As life becomes more complex, more impersonal, more mechanised and synthetic, it is surely important that we see and understand these things. If we can gain from them and use our enjoyment to give life, colour, romance and beauty to our homes at the same time we will be fulfilling ourselves.

Rhoicissus rhomboidea trailing across a wall

2 PLANTS AND FLOWERS FOR LONG LIFE

We all know that any arrangement of fresh cut flowers, however beautiful, is destined to die. But having spent time and talent on their arrangement and sometimes money on their purchase, it seems a pity not to try to keep them fresh and lovely for as long as possible.

The life of a flower must depend originally upon the plant which was its source. When we have to buy our flowers we cannot control this source although we can decide whether or not to make our purchase, and in the next chapter I give a few hints on buying flowers and plants which will ensure greater value and longer life from them.

There is one basic reason why a flower or stem hangs its head, droops and flags after it has been cut from the plant. It simply is not getting sufficient water up the stem to balance its loss of moisture through leaves or petals. So we must take steps wherever possible both to increase the intake of water and to decrease the transpiration rate.

When cutting flowers from the garden for decoration in the home it is always wise to reduce to a minimum the time lag between actually cutting the flower and placing it in water. So take a bucket with you and in it make sure that there are at least three inches of water. Place the flowers in this immediately they are cut and in almost every case the flowers will not subsequently flag. If they do flag, it will probably be because an air lock has formed in the tissues carrying moisture upwards from the plant's roots. In this case cut away (preferably under water) the bottom half inch or so of stem, as this is probably the location of the air lock. The flowers should then be able to absorb the water.

In some flowers, particularly those with woody stems such as chrysanthemums or branches of blossom, this air lock may have travelled some way up the stem and it is necessary to force water up the stem. In this case use the boiling water treatment. Pour two or three inches of boiling water into a can or bucket and place the stem

Euphorbia pulcherima arranged in a flat bowl

ends of the wilting flowers in this. Leave until the water is cool and then arrange the flowers in fresh cold water. The air lock will have been forced out by the boiling water.

Common sense will suggest that this somewhat drastic treatment should not be used on tiny, delicate flowers such as violets, primroses, pansies and the like, and in fact it should neither be used on any flowers grown from bulbs or corms. So never try it on daffodils, tulips, hyacinths, lilies, gladioli, anemones or the like. If there is trouble with these it is probably because they have been cut too close to the bulb, and any white portion at the base of the stem should be cut away to enable the flower to drink.

On the other hand, if an arrangement has been completed with the flowers apparently in good condition yet a few hours later some stems begin inexplicably to flag, the hot water treatment will normally bring these back to a healthy, turgid state. Take out the wilting stems from the arrangement and give them the hot water treatment before replacing them. This should do the trick.

Never cut flowers when they are too immature. Yet on the other hand flowers in bud obviously will have a longer indoor life and flowers which have fulfilled their basic function and spilled their pollen will have passed their best and have little useful decorative life ahead of them.

An attractive arrangement of cut roses in a glass bowl

Plants and flowers for long life

Roses in bud may look very tender and lovely, but if their calyces, the green protective covering, have not opened and begun to curl backwards, they will never take water. Daffodils must have reached the goose-neck stage, be bending their heads downwards, before they are cut. A little experience will soon indicate the best time to cut flowers from the garden so that they will have the longest possible decorative life in the home.

One group of plants presents a special problem, and are those plants that exude a milky latex from their stems when cut. These include all poppies and the gorgeous *Euphorbia pulcherrima*, or poinsettia, until recently seen mainly at Christmas but now available in the shops the whole year round. It is necessary to stop this "bleeding" before arranging the flowers. The best way, of course, is never to allow it to take place in the first instance. This means arranging the flowers while still on their roots. You can pull up poppies from the soil, wash the roots clear and clean and then arrange them as they are, and poinsettia plants can be knocked from their pots, soil shaken and then washed off and arranged again on their roots.

This is not always possible, and where flowers are to be cut to different lengths for arrangement it is obviously out of the question, so we have to make arrangements to stop the bleeding from each stem that we use. The flow of latex from the wound will cease if it is caused to coagulate

Pots of cyclamen on an occasional table

and this can be done if the stem end is plunged in dry sand or in powdered charcoal. Alternatively, hold the oozing stem end over a candle flame or a gas jet for a few seconds until it is charred.

Some flowers, mainly annuals, are so small and delicate that any kind of over-handling will bruise them or give them a slightly weary appearance. Some of these can be drawn through a basin or sink of clean cold water, any excess gently shaken off them then arranged, still moist. Or alternatively they can be given an almost invisible spray of clean water from an atomiser. This will reduce their transpiration rate for some hours.

Never stand a bowl of flowers in strong sunlight, in a draught or where heat from fire or radiator can strike them. Again, never stand them in such a position that a night frost can cause damage. It is sometimes easy in winter to have a lovely vase of flowers in a window and thoughtlessly to close the curtains at night, leaving the flowers on the ledge between window and curtain. The room heat is prevented from warming the flowers because of the curtain, the frost gets in and the flowers are killed.

In winter our rooms tend to heat up in the evenings and because heat rises flowers set high on a pedestal or in a wall vase sometimes suffer from this excess of heat. So if you normally set flowers high in your living rooms, bring them to a lower level earlier in the day before they become affected.

Many of the suggestions put forward here apply also to house plants. In general terms keep most of them out of direct sunlight (except, of course, cacti and succulents, most of which revel in the light and heat) and out of draughts from windows and direct heat from fires and radiators. Bright light is helpful to some plants, particularly those in flower or with variegated or coloured foliage, so place them near a good light source but not in direct sunlight. A light net or nylon curtain will filter out the strongest elements of sunlight and a good place for plants is often a shelf or stand at right angles to a south facing window. A position directly in a north or east window suits plants which require a constant supply of good light, for any sun reaching them directly will be of so weak a nature and of so brief a duration that it can do no real harm.

Plants and flowers for long life

All plants need some light, but a few can be made to flourish in surprisingly dark surroundings. As a general rule it is possible to say that foliage plants with dark, fleshy and glossy leaves will take less light than others. These plants include the rubber plant, *Ficus elastica* (but not the variegated forms), the Swiss cheese plant, *Monstera deliciosa,* and the goose foot plant, *Syngonium vellozianum*. The last is particularly useful for dark corners, as it bears gleaming white, lily-like "flowers", really bracts.

Fortunately there are elements in the normal incandescent lighting that we employ in our homes that are acceptable as a light source by plants, so where natural light from windows is limited artificial light helps to provide illumination necessary for the photosynthetic processes of many house plants.

But our rooms are normally not only darker than the great outdoors in which our flowers and plants naturally grow, they are unfortunately drier. The degree of humidity enjoyed by many house plants would be quite intolerable to us as humans. Both house plants and flowers will manage to live for limited periods in the arid atmosphere enjoyed by humans, but to lengthen their life it is often helpful to give them some slight degree of artificial humidity.

Codiaeum (Croton)

Group of begonias

Plants and flowers for long life

In summer windows are normally left open and the difference between indoor and outdoor atmosphere is slight. But in winter we like our homes to be warmer than outdoors and because we heat them they become drier. So we should take steps in winter to increase indoor humidity and fortunately this is neither a difficult matter nor does it cause any discomfort. Indeed, a slight increase in indoor humidity is beneficial both to human skin and to furniture, which (like our skin!) tends to crack and warp if it becomes too dry.

The simplest means of providing a slightly greater degree of humidity in the home is merely to place one or two shallow pans of water about the house in convenient and inconspicuous places. A few flowers arranged in a large bowl will do the trick. Until recently I used for some years a long, copper trough, actually a wine cooler, for this purpose. To make it slightly more decorative I filled this with gaily coloured sea shells and kept it always filled with water. This provided a surprising amount of extra humidity, which I always keep under review and strict control by means of a small and inexpensive humidity gauge.

It is possible to buy several types of humidifiers, which are merely means of sending modest amounts of moist air into the indoor atmosphere. Personally I now use long, narrow china troughs which are filled with water daily and hung behind the radiators. These can increase the relative humidity by up to ten degrees in a few hours and I estimate that the total amount of additional moisture I send into the air to be as much as two gallons a week for the entire house.

Mixed arrangement of indoor plants in an attractive ceramic container

In the warm, dry atmosphere of our homes in winter it is also helpful to give most house plants a light spray with clean, tepid water once a day. Tiny sprays are available for this purpose at very small cost. Only a slight film over the foliage is necessary, but even this can cause marking and damage to furnishings, so either protect the surroundings before spraying or move plants to a safe place.

Still another useful means of giving plants the extra humidity they require is by means of plunge pots. By this I mean standing the plant pot inside another and larger container, preferably decorative, with the space between the two pots packed with peat or some similar absorbent material. If this is kept constantly moist evaporation will send a modest amount of moisture into the air, its most immediate location being around the foliage of the plant itself, to its great benefit.

For certain very special plants it is possible to carry this practice even further and provide occasional "humidity baths". Saintpaulias, or African violets, for example, flower best under comparatively humid conditions and given this treatment on occasion can be induced to produce their charming little flowers the winter through. Stand the plant in its pot inside a slightly larger bowl and then stand this inside a considerably larger bowl or basin. Fill the space between the latter two with boiling water. The steam will arise and envelop the entire plant, not so hot that it can cause damage, but moist enough to give a real boost to the immediate humidity surrounding it.

Begonias in a copper bowl. Also suitable for hanging baskets

This matter of increasing humidity in the home during the winter months is really important, not only because our homes are drier at this time in relation to outdoor levels, but because most plants require and receive less water at their roots in winter. Nearly all house plants should be watered only sparingly in winter, mainly because their rate of growth is slower at this period, but also to keep the roots warm and snug.

It is not generally realised that the watering of pot plants fulfills two functions: the provision of vital

Mixed bowl of house plants on a low bookcase

moisture and the provision of vital air. When water is poured on to the surface soil of a plant in a pot it rushes through the soil and eventually out through the hole at the base of the pot. By rushing through the soil like this it drags after it air from the atmosphere. If pot plants are over-watered all the air spaces in the soil are filled with moisture and the roots cannot breathe. More plants are killed by over-watering than by any means and it is vitally important to understand this double function of watering.

Never allow any plants to "paddle", to stand in a saucer or other container with water, except for a few minutes. When watering a plant it is frequently found that the moisture rushes through the soil, collects in the saucer and then, after a few minutes, is absorbed again into the pot. If this does not happen, empty away any excess moisture, as otherwise it will mean that the soil is saturated and no air spaces exist.

Just as more plants are killed by over-watering than any other means of mismanagement, so most house plants are also given too much food. When brought from the nursery for sale to the public all house plants are approaching their peak of condition and the aim of the owner should be to bring the plant gently and gradually to this peak and to maintain it in this condition as long as possible.

All plants from reputable growers reach the public growing in soil containing sufficient nutrients for several months and a "new" plant should not require feeding for at least four months. The only exception to this rule is for flowering plants. These use up so much of their energy in producing flowers that they benefit from regular feeding at this time.

Over-feeding rushes a plant too quickly into maturity and hastens its eventual death. It also results in quick growth, which often means that a plant outgrows its situation in the home. The object and aim of all house-plant tending should be to maintain the plant in peak condition and at a slow rate of growth for as long as possible.

Flowers, too, continue to grow and to mature even after they have been cut from the parent stem, and our aim should be to reduce the rate of growth as far as possible. Never change the water daily in a flower arrangement; merely top up the level when necessary. If the water becomes foul and smelly this is either because the plant tissue under water is decomposing or because bacterial activity in the water has been hastened by strong light. So keep containers as well as plants out of sunlight, particularly when made of glass, and always trim from the stems which go under water all leaves or other excess of vegetable matter which will decompose.

An aspirin or a penny in the water serves only to delay bacterial activity slightly and the so-called cut flower preservatives available consist mainly of ingredients to delay bacterial activity plus some form of plant food. This is usually some type of glucose. A lump of sugar or a teaspoonful of honey will normally be just as useful.

Some flowers, particularly bulb flowers, last better in shallow than in deep water. If gladioli snap their stems and become brittle, if tulips snake about with curving stems, it is because they are getting too much water. Two or three inches is quite sufficient, but make sure that this is replaced to this level each day.

Other flowers, sweet peas for example, must never be picked while wet or sprayed while in the vase or the lovely flowers will become pitted and spotted and they will quickly rot.

A bowl of cut gladioli

African violets (Saintpaulia ionantha)
This attractive little plant bears masses of flowers, single or double, depending on the variety.

Columbine (Aquilegia)
There is quite a wide range of named varieties, all of which are good for cut-flower arrangements.

Begonias are among the most striking flowers for growing in pots indoors. Several varieties are excellent for hanging baskets.

The flower heads of three varieties of buddleia. Long spikes of this shrub are excellent for cut-flower arrangements, especially in the summer.

3 BUYING PLANTS AND FLOWERS

To the eternal chagrin of the commercial florist few of us deliberately leave our homes and go to the shops with the intention of buying some flowers or a pot plant or two. Nearly all flower and plant buying is done on impulse, except, of course, those bought as gifts.

This is really a pity, for our flower and plant decorations could be both more effective and more economical if we looked around the home quite deliberately before we went off to the stores, to decide which of our existing flowers and plants were in good enough condition to keep and which required replacement, to decide that a splash of colour was necessary in that corner or that a tall and striking plant would look particularly effective in the corner by the new standard lamp.

But whether purchases are made on impulse or as a deliberate policy, it is obviously wise to demand good value for money, and this means fresh flowers. Unfortunately, flowers that are in the peak of condition are too old for us; they should be approaching this peak. So look

Mixed arrangement of spring flowers

for slightly immature flowers, crisp and almost hard in appearance.

Bulb flowers should be still in bud, just beginning to open. Their stem ends should not be curled or brown. If they are white at the ends cut this portion away before giving them a drink. Anemones should not be too tight in bud or they may not open. Petal colour should be bright and the stamens in the centre should be fairly tight. No pollen should be visible.

Chrysanthemums and carnations should still be just a little tight in the centre, indicating that there are still some petals to unfold. Outer petals should still have the bloom colour, should never be brown and soft. Make sure stems are strong, but don't worry too much about bruised or brown stem ends unless they are slimy. Stem ends in any case should be cut away before you give the flowers a drink when you get home.

Mixed arrangement of chrysanthemums and beech leaves

Foliage often fails before the flowers, so look at the leaves carefully. If they are merely flagged it is probable that they will crisp up on being given a drink. If they are brown or brittle reject the flowers.

Remember that there will be a difference in flowers bought from the town florist or from market or nursery. The florist usually buys his flowers in the early morning, anything up to a day after they have been cut. He takes them back to the shop, trims stem ends and stands them in water. So to some extent they have been conditioned for you before you get them home yourself. In the market the flowers are only a few hours younger but they have not been conditioned; they are sold straight from the box so may look a little limp and tired, but basically they are just as good (with proper handling) as those from the florist. Examine carefully any flowers you may buy at the nursery or the farm gate. They may be rejects not good

Arrangement of carnations in a pottery bowl

Display of anemones, grape hyacinths and shadow leaves in a blue glass

enough for sending to market or they may have stood in water but in hot sunlight all day at the farm gate.

Whenever you buy flowers make sure that they are properly wrapped before you leave the shop, particularly in winter. This means that the wet stems must be protected but even more important, the flower heads should be completely covered with paper. In the half hour it may take you to reach home sunshine or icy blasts can so damage the tender petals as to reduce substantially their expectation of life.

When buying plants, too, make sure that the entire plant is protected, not just the flower pot, for this is covered merely to avoid you getting soiled. Many plants today are sold in special packs and these are excellent and normally a sign of a good plant.

Never buy a wilted plant. It may never recover. Once again look for crisp foliage, undamaged, clean and preferably shiny. Look particularly at the growing shoot or shoots, for damage here, possibly caused in transport, can mean that the plant will not develop.

If you see a single pest of any kind, or any evidence of pest damage, reject the plant. Turn over a few leaves and look on the undersides, examine the joints with the main stems.

If you are buying a flowering plant make sure that there are plenty of strong, healthy, fat young buds ready to produce a succession of flowers. See that the flowers have good colour and are not spotted by spraying. Feel the soil surface and make sure it is moist. Do not buy a plant with roots showing at the top of the pot or through the drainage hole at the base; the first indicates that the plant needs re-potting, the second that root damage has possibly been caused when the plant was lifted from the nursery bench.

When buying a large plant make sure that it is adequately and securely staked and supported. Examine the places where it is attached to the stake and make quite sure that no damage has been caused to the stems by over-tight tying.

When you get your flowers or plants home condition them immediately. Cut the stem ends of your flowers and place them in deep water for at least an hour or two before arranging them. Water all pot plants thoroughly, pre-

Mixed arrangement of daffodils, hyacinths, croton, ivy and scindapsus in a bowl

ferably by holding the entire pot under water until bubbles cease to rise from the soil surface, and then allow to drain before placing in position.

Many foliage pot plants look a little stiff and formal when first bought. This is largely because they have been attached to their cane or stake too firmly so they will travel well from nursery to market or shop. Loosen or undo these ties where you feel a trail could hang prettily or where the general effect would look better if the foliage were to be "fluffed out" a little.

Remember that once you have bought them, your flowers and plants are your own responsibility. Look after them and imprint your own personality on the way you use them for decorating your home.

4 POTS AND CONTAINERS

Every plant growing in the home should be stood in some kind of container, primarily to avoid damage to furniture. It is possible to buy matching decorative pots and saucers, usually ceramic, and many pot plant holders in wire or wicker work combine their own saucers, usually metal. But the trouble with so many purpose made pot plant containers is simply that they are too small. The containers themselves reveal the ugly upper portions of the flower pot and the saucers either fit so tightly that there is no space for excess water or they do not fit at all.

Any receptacle that is waterproof, aesthetically pleasing and large enough can be used as a pot plant holder. Plants can look very attractive growing out of a bowl, a vase, a copper saucepan, a teapot, a Victorian wash bowl, an ashtray, a coal scuttle or anything else that suits the decor of the home and the shape, colour and texture of the plant. If the receptacle is not waterproof it can easily be lined with plastic sheeting or kitchen foil.

Low, saucer-like containers are both convenient and suitable in many cases, but they limit the decorative possibilities open to us and render more difficult the

Spring flowers displayed in a white Lennox vase

minimal attentions required by the plants. Much better to use containers large enough to pack insulating and water absorbing materials between the plant pot and the container, for these materials absorb excess moisture applied when watering and keep plant roots cool in summer, warm in winter.

Arrangement of flowers, vegetables and fruits in a copper jelly mould

Too seldom seen are tall containers, in which the plant itself sits in or near the top on a base of peat, sand, Florapak or even crumpled newspaper. If the plant is raised high, at least six inches, then it gains in dignity and importance. Tall growing plants such as an aechmea or a cyperus are much more imposing if raised in this manner and trailers and scramblers such as tradescantia are so much more attractive if their long stems can cascade downwards free of obstruction for a few more inches.

Beware, however, of using tall plant containers if the plant itself is too tall, for the entire ensemble can then be top heavy and apt to fall when brushed against. The tall blades of sansevieria, for example, can grow to three feet or more and need a really solid base. Ballasting a tall container with moist sand can help in this case.

Containers for flower arrangements are even less limited than those for plants, because even the smallest plant demands a comparatively large aperture at the top, whereas the single stem of a perfect rose, for example, demands an opening only the size of a pencil. Otherwise the rules are much the same: the container must be

An attractive arrangement of amaryllis in a shell bowl

waterproof, pleasing and suited to both flowers and room decoration. Anything, from formal cut glass and silver down to the humblest kitchen receptacle, is permissible. Nothing is barred.

But watch out for the twin dangers of suitability and proportion. For example, many jugs make excellent containers for flower arrangements. But whereas a slim, modern, elegant and sophisticated glass cocktail jug may be suitable for a single stem or even a complex arrangement of gladioli, a humbler, fatter, pottery or earthenware jug would be demanded by roses or tulips and any jug would have the wrong proportions for small and tender flowers such as pansies.

Beware, too, the patterned container unless colours and design match exactly the flowers it is to contain. Over-ornate or highly coloured containers generally draw attention to themselves instead of the flowers and only the expert can bring them into harmony. Cut glass is often more beautiful alone than as a flower container.

If you have a container of beautiful shape but the wrong colour, try painting it with easily removed poster paints.

Consider the shape of the arrangement you intend to create before deciding on the vase or container. A tall and upstanding arrangement demands either a tall container or a low, flat one. A circular bowl would look all wrong. Bear in mind one of the few basic rules of flower arrangement: the tallest stem should always be not less than one and a half times the height of the container, though it can be much more.

Bromeliads growing in part of a tree trunk

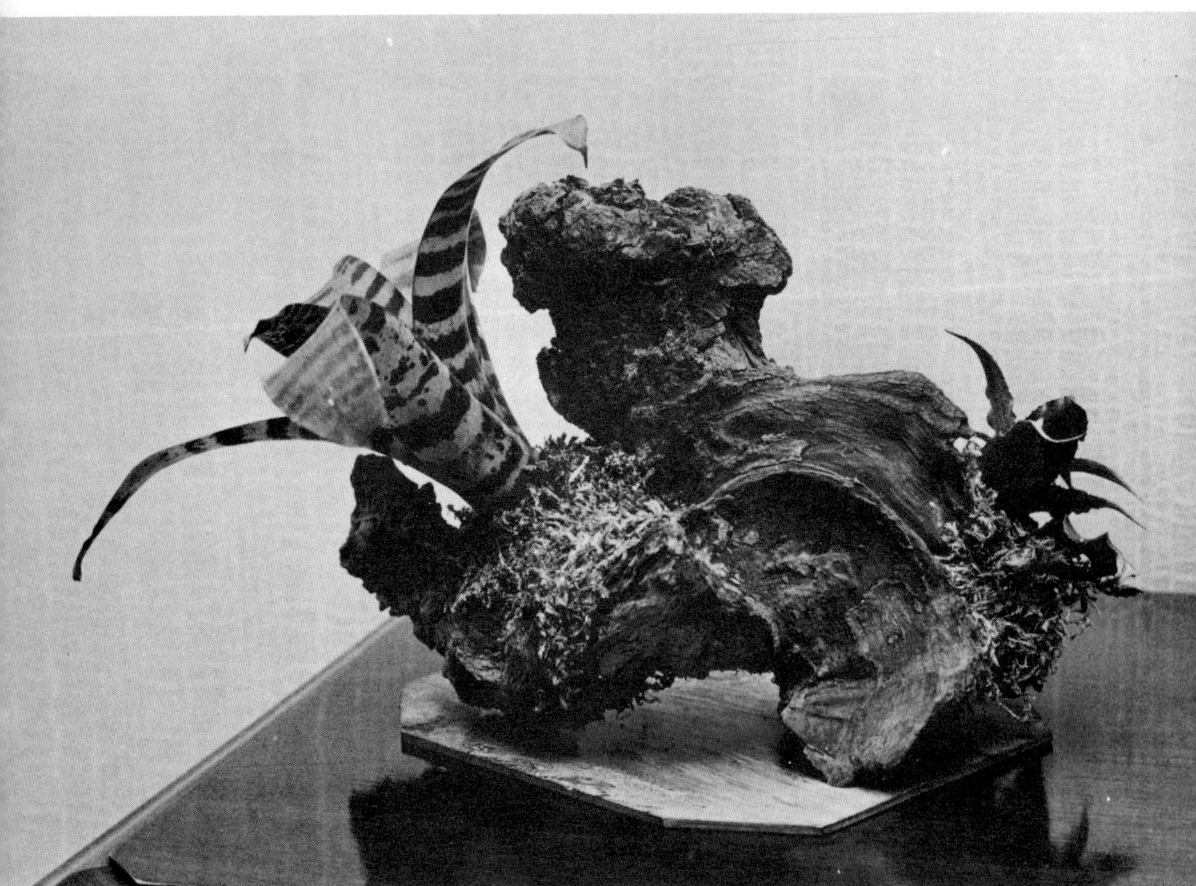

Various plant containers sited in a window; note the copper tea urn at bottom left

Pots and containers

Consider the texture of your container as well as its shape and colour. Texture is of particular importance with different types of flowers. Soft textures such as pottery, earthenware, wood and even some plastics, suit soft and simple flowers, though even unsophisticated copper and pewter also fit into this class. More elegant and formal flowers, such as so many bought from the florist store, blend more happily with china, glass, silver and similar textures.

Textures also matter with plants, and where a planted arrangement is to be made, including several plants of differing families, the texture should always be soft and informal. For a planted group has affinities with natural growth in garden or woodland and where, to take a close example, one could make an attractive group of plants in a plain, modest, straightforward copper wine cooler, the same plants in an ornate silver champagne bucket would look ill at ease.

Planting direct into glazed or otherwise waterproof containers poses certain problems, and it is a practice generally frowned upon by experts. It can, however, be done quite successfully and I have myself some plants grown like this for up to ten years and still happy in their homes.

The major problem is one of drainage, for as we have already seen, plants need not only moisture at their roots but air also. The answer to this problem is to choose a container deep enough for a substantial drainage layer, at least two inches deep, preferably more. This goes in first, of course. It can consist of broken crocks, pebbles, shingle, anything like this that is not toxic and will freely admit water. But as water is likely to lie in this layer for some time and may become sour and smelly, add a few nuggets of charcoal, freely and cheaply available from all chemist or drug stores. On top of this drainage layer place your soil, but to avoid this being washed down into the drainage and so preventing it from doing its work, separate the two layers with a piece of rag, burlap or sacking.

The soil mixture used can be from the garden or one of the several proprietary mixtures available from all garden stores. It should be fairly rich, open and well drained in texture, yet sufficiently absorbent to hold its moisture. Garden soil should generally be enriched by leaf mould, peat and sharp sand.

Knock the plants from their pots by holding three fingers on top of the soil, turning the plant upside down and tapping the plant pot sharply on some hard surface. The entire root ball will fall out into the fingers. Loosen the soil slightly in this root ball and gently spread out the roots in the soil of the new container, sifting the soil around them so that each root hair is in intimate contact with the soil and no air pockets are left. Firm the soil around the plant with the knuckles. Continue with the other plants in the same fashion, being careful to leave sufficient space between soil level and the rim of the container to allow for easy watering.

A Victorian lamp standard adapted as a plant container

Once planted, water the container thoroughly and then leave it to become almost dry before watering again. Remember that the drainage layer you have placed at the base of the container will act as a miniature reservoir and keep the soil moist for long periods, so do not water so lavishly or so frequently that it overflows and so fails in its function.

Roses and aucuba leaves attractively arranged in a ceramic bowl

5 PLACING DECORATIONS IN THE HOME

As I have already indicated, all decoration of the home (or the office!) with flowers and plants should be carried out with a definite purpose in mind. The decorations should be functional. The function is generally to beautify, but it can also be to impress, to welcome, to disguise, to hide, to emphasise, to link, to point to a specific object such as a picture, or to serve as an exclamation mark!

It is not the purpose of this book to deal with decorations outside the home or in the garden, but perhaps it is permissible to say that plants in the porch or beside the front door always serve both to welcome the guest and to implant on him or her the immediate reaction that the home owners are cultured, gracious, warm hearted, generous, intellectual and financially comfortable, an impression we would all like to give.

In just the same way there should always be some decoration inside the hallway to be immediately apparent when the visitor crosses the threshold. Although this should, in theory, be in an advancing colour, red, orange or yellow, practical problems in the way of available light, surrounding decorations, sheer availability of flower and plant materials and the like make this less important than the existence of the welcoming token, regardless of colour. Certainly flowers are to be preferred in this position to plants, for they project a more personal image, but again plants are better than a blank wall.

In the living room there should be only one decoration of dominance and significance. The others, if there is space, should be subservient to the one major decoration, which should be striking enough to demand immediate attention. It should set the atmosphere for the room, either warm and vibrant or cool and restful, but in any case should blend happily with the major decorative colours or pick out and echo some important decorative theme. Each of the other decorations, whether of flowers or plants or both, should bear some relation to the major

A display of cut flowers and potted plants at the end of a hall

effect, consciously or unconsciously, in colour, texture or theme, but unless there is some obvious relationship not in shape or materials. By this I mean that the only excuse for close similarity will be a pair of almost identical arrangements on each side of a fireplace, or perhaps a large decoration on the tallest of a nest of coffee tables with a smaller replica at the other end on the smallest.

Yet speaking of coffee tables, to avoid the possible discomfort and discomfiture of guests, never place any type of flower or plant arrangement so that it impedes the progress or movement of any person acting normally. Place a beautiful flower arrangement close enough to be admired and examined, but never so close that anyone must walk around it or take care lest it be disturbed.

In the dining room the only function of flowers or plants is to enhance the appearance of the room or the table setting. Flowers or plants should not be dominant. They must never be strongly scented. They should blend with table, cloth, mats or china rather than contrast and so draw overdue attention to themselves. They must

A truly imaginative display of carnations. This example shows very clearly how simple pieces of driftwood can be used in displays.

A pot of ''Pink Cherub'' chrysanthemums. It makes an attractive feature indoors or in a conservatory.

never be so tall when placed upon the dining table that guests must crane their heads to see each other, nor so striking on the sideboard that eyes and thoughts wander away to them during dinner table conversation.

Placing decorations in the home

Always consider available light when placing a flower arrangement in position. Where a stylised and elegant arrangement of almost black tulips will look striking and dramatic in bright light against a white wall, it will be practically invisible in a dark corner. Flowers and plants will be visible largely in silhouette in a north and east window on a dark day and may be bleached and almost transparent in a south or west window when the sun is bright.

For variegated or flowering plants a south or west aspect is necessary to maintain good colour in foliage or flowers, but except for cacti, succulents and a very few special plants the sun should not be allowed to strike them directly for more than a few minutes at a time. No flower arrangement should ever be stood in direct sunlight, though here, fortunately, few arrangements are large enough to stand for long in the moving rays of the sun.

In artificial light at night-time white is always excellent. Yellow tends to become white, so add yellow accessories. Orange and the pink tints take on additional colour under incandescent lighting. Blues and purples become blacker. Remember these points when arranging flowers during the day time for an evening party, and bear in mind, too, the fact that if you dine by candle light all of your flowers except the lightest in hue will drop several degrees down the light scale when you switch off the electricity. Candle light may be kind and attractive to humans, but it can make some flower colours almost disappear.

Red, orange and yellow are warm colours, strident and advancing. Use them in a cold room or at the end where it is long and narrow. Do not use them too boldly in a small room as they demand too much attention and tend to kill every other colour.

Blue is a cold colour, splendid for hot summer days, which gives the impression of receding. So place blue flowers against the wall of a small room and that wall will appear to be further away than it actually is.

One or two tall arrangements, either upright themselves or standing on a torchère or some similar tall and upright piece of furniture will make the room look taller. And low spreading arrangements will do the opposite and make a high ceiling appear to be lower.

If you wish to hide or disguise an ugly or shabby piece of furniture, place a vivid flower arrangement or a striking plant before or beside it to catch and hold the eye. If you wish to conceal a dull and uninteresting view plant up a gay and vivid indoor window box so your eyes are drawn to this and not out of the window. If you wish to draw attention to a special painting create a flower arrangement to be placed nearby that makes use of the major hues in the painting or even takes its cue from the line, pattern or proportions. Buy or paint the flower container to match the picture frame.

One of the more dispiriting sections of the modern living room today is the fireplace. If used at all this fulfills its function of providing heat and attention only for a few months of the year and is otherwise left vacant, a

Hedera helix and syngonium displayed on a wrought iron fitted table

blank eye staring out into the room, a pointless focal point. This is a wonderful place to arrange plants, always in the summer and today frequently in the winter too, for central heating systems have left the fireplace empty and without point or function.

It can retain its former position as a focal point if it

Tiered urns, an attractive if unusual style of displaying indoor plants

is filled with plants, and fortunately its construction makes it ideal for this purpose. It is large enough to take several plants. It is at floor level which means that most plants placed there can be seen at the level at which they normally grow and so appear unusually attractive. It has been made of materials which are impervious to moisture, which means that we can mass plants there without the restrictions of fearing for water drips, which means that we can spray them regardless of possible harm to furnishings and that we can tend them without having to move bulky furniture or squeeze between chairs and the window sill.

First block the aperture to the chimney. Where central heating has been installed it is probable that this will already have been done. Otherwise there is apt to be a considerable and damaging draught through the plants and up the chimney and on certain occasions a reverse draught coming down the chimney. This can cause real harm to the plants.

Bear in mind also the fact that while the fireplace itself is not being used, neither are its accessories, coal box, log basket, ash pan and the like. All of these make

A group of indoor plants in a wicker-work container on a low windowsill

admirable plant containers and carry out both a decorative and a functional purpose.

Normally the fireplace is set well away from the windows, which means that light will not be sufficient for most flowering or variegated plants. There are plenty of others. Space suffices for tall growing plants, sprawlers and chunky specimens.

In the hot days of summer opportunity offers itself for making the fireplace a cool and refreshing reservoir, a centre of green, growing peace. Make a real feature of it. Don't just dump a series of plants on the hearth with a "this is where we can put them" attitude, but design the display with taste and cunning. Wedge plants in place with attractively gnarled pieces of driftwood or cork bark. Fill in spaces with moist and humidifying moss. Set a tall growing philodendron or cissus to climb up and

smother the wall. Lodge a starry cryptanthus or two on upward leaning pieces of bark, growing the way so many of them do in their native jungles. Place on the floor one or two nidulariums or neoregelias so you can enjoy the rare opportunity of looking immediately into their vivid scarlet or magenta centres. Or arrange a pattern of African violets in the blues, pinks and whites to give a tender and delicate touch to what is so often a hard, arid and heat-bleached area.

And although the actual source of heat in winter has been removed from the fireplace to radiators, do not neglect these as home decoration. Of course plants and flowers must not be allowed to come into direct contact with their heated surfaces, but in general it is safe to say that the warmth they produce is of less danger to flowers and plants than the movement of air, heated air, that they generate. Many plants will grow quite happily near the warmth of a radiator so long as they are protected from the current of hot air which circulates in the vicinity. Many radiators are, or can be, fitted with shelves to deflect air currents. Use of these shelves in no way lessens the quantity of heat produced; it merely moves the current of hot air in another direction.

ican violets.
se striking
wers will
ance any
m in the house

Mixed arrangement of house plants as a central feature in a bay window

Monstera, ivy and tradescantia attractively displayed in an antique copper urn. The copper spirit lamp on the left holds a *Ficus radicans*

Some plants which are not too wide spreading can actually stand on these radiator shelves and indeed gain benefit from the gentle bottom heat they receive this way. This can, in fact, be an excellent spot for the germination of some seeds in late winter or for the production of new plants from cuttings.

In late winter, too, a position near a radiator can be ideal for the coaxing into early leaf and blossom of a large branch of prunus, forsythia or hazel. If the radiator is encouraged to produce humidity as well as warmth any of these branches and several others will quickly react to the feeling of false spring and put out tender green leaves or delicately coloured flowers. Several bulb flowers and even tender primroses can be brought indoors in pots to stand at the foot of such a "tree" and with their pots hidden with moss they will also help to provide the humidity necessary to bring on a premature spring scene indoors while the bleak boughs of winter still bend to the bitter winds outside.

So many hallways have tall ceilings leading up to the next floor that this is an excellent place for a tall, yet wall-hugging arrangement of this kind. This location is helpful, too, in that it is generally less warm than the living rooms yet still having a temperature considerably higher than that outdoors. Natural humidity will also be higher than that in the living rooms because of the frequently opened door.

And if instead of being vertical and flat the required arrangement is to be horizontal and flat, say for a long, narrow shelf or mantelpiece, plenty of opportunity still exists. An L-shaped arrangement of cut flowers can be made on one side, L-shaped both sides or a central low arrangement can be made spreading out in both directions. Flat branches of green beech can set the scene and sketch the dimensions with almost any flowers in season and readily available to provide the colour. If plants are used instead trails of ivy, *Philodendron scandens,* cissus or rhoicissus can be used both for the horizontal and the vertical with dracaena or cordyline to act as a centre piece and pivot.

But do not concentrate all your arrangements of plants and flowers only in the public rooms. Bedrooms too require decorating, though generally in a less vivid and more personal strain. If you take morning tea or coffee to your guest, always place on the tray a tiny posy or nosegay of flowers, perhaps arranged in an egg cup or some similarly small, convenient and intimate container. The bathroom, so long as water is not heated by gas, is a splendid place for certain house plants, for the humidity is generally high and the temperature comparatively steady. African violets do well in bathrooms and the heart-shaped foliage of *Philodendron scandens* can be trailed attractively to decorate what is so frequently a somewhat bleak and austere room.

The kitchen again is frequently warm and humid and so long as they do not get in the way of necessary activities plants frequently feel at home there. The most obvious plants for the kitchen are obviously herbs and parsley, chives, mint, tarragon and chervil will all grow well in most kitchens. It is best to prepare duplicate pots of each, maintaining one indoors and one out and changing them as they become used or as they begin to fade under indoor conditions. Keep them in as bright a position as possible and never forget to give them plenty of water when this appears necessary.

This photograph shows how pewter mugs can be used to display plants

6 INDIVIDUAL PLANTS AND THEIR CULTURE

All house and flowering plants today reach us bearing labels giving their botanical names, sometimes with brief details of the care they should receive. The following list of plants for the home is concerned less with their cultivation as plants than with their care, position, use and decorative value in the home. Although they are listed under their botanical names they are also cross-referenced under their popular or colloquial names where these exist. This list does not claim to be exhaustive; it concentrates on those plants most likely to be found indoors and those that give good decorative value for considerable periods, though even some of these may require a period in the greenhouse or out of doors to recover from their spell of duty inside the home.

Aaron's beard, see **SAXIFRAGA STOLONIFERA**

ADIANTUM CUNEATUM (Maidenhair fern) A fern with small, delicate green leaves carried on wiry black stems. Keep cool, moist and in a shaded position free of draughts. Use with other ferns in an empty summer fireplace or in a temporary plant arrangement for the dinner table. Delicate.

Adiantum (Maidenhair fern)

Aechmea
(Greek vase plant)

Individual plants

AECHMEA RHODOCYANEA (Greek vase plant) A bromeliad with grey-green strap-like leaves radiating from a central point forming the "vase". Keep this always filled with water but do not water soil surface. Flowers at maturity, a tall, spiky stem bearing pink, blue and violet flowers, long lasting. A tough, easy and tolerant plant particularly suited to a solo role.

African violet, see **SAINTPAULIA IONANTHA**

AGLAONEMA (Chinese evergreen) Most popular are *A. angustifolium, A. commutatum* and *A. robelinii,* all with variations of green leaves striped, flecked or blotched with white, cream, pale green or silver. Keep warm, excellent for centrally heated homes. Likes light shade, plenty of water in summer but barely moist in winter. Use either alone or in big, bold groupings. Usually long lived and fairly easy.

Aglaonema
(Chinese evergreen)

Left, Anthurium (Flamingo flower). Right, Aphelandra (Saffron spike)

ANTHURIUM (Flamingo flower, palette plant, piggy tail plant) Usually either *A. andreanum* or *A. scherzerianum,* with dark green, glossy leaves and shield-shaped shiny flowers, scarlet, pink or white, bearing the characteristic upright or curled "piggy tail". Flowers are long-lasting, unusual, decorative. Keep warm, moist and in good light. Useful as a specimen plant or in a group, where the flowers usually stand above and brighten the more general green.

APHELANDRA SQUARROSA LOUISAE (Saffron spike, zebra plant) Carries large, green, white-banded leaves topped with a cockscomb of orange bracts bearing yellow flowers. Striking and beautiful but difficult to keep for long. A specimen plant when in good condition and capable of being disguised in a group when lower leaves begin to fall. Keep warm, moist, out of direct sun.

ARAUCARIA EXCELSA (Norfolk Island pine) A miniature pine tree, tough, decorative, quick growing. Will grow in sun or shade. Plenty of water in spring is demanded but less in winter. A good plant for grouping, either with light lovers or shady characters such as ferns.

ASPIDISTRA ELATIOR (Cast iron plant, parlour palm) Dark green, spear shaped individual leaves. There

Calathea

is also a variegated form. Easy and tolerant, growing under almost any conditions. Useful mainly in groups of any kind and suitable for mixing with almost any other plants. Leaves dry well and are popular for flower arrangements. Plenty of water in summer, less in winter. Stands heat or cold, sun or shade.

AZALEA INDICA Popular flowering plant, usually pink, red or white. Temporary and difficult but very lovely. Keep root ball always moist and occasionally spray foliage. Keep warm and in light shade. Good specimens are magnificent alone; smaller plants look well either grouped together or with other flowering or foliage plants.

Baby's tears, see **HELXINE SOLEIROLLII**

BEGONIA Both flowering and foliage species popular and useful as house plants with a wide range of both, all highly decorative, long lasting and comparatively easy. Generally keep warm, moist, out of draughts and away from all smoke and fumes. Most like positions in light shade. Use together in groups rather than with other plants, mixing colours, shapes and textures in the one family to obtain greatest impact. Some foliage types with almost metallic leaves make striking specimens.

BELOPERONE GUTTATA (Shrimp plant) Unusual miniature shrub with flowers similar in colour, shape and size to shrimps. Give full light for good colour and keep always just moist in fairly warm surroundings. Large and fully flowered specimens good alone, perhaps in the kitchen; younger and smaller plants do well in groups of foliage plants to give a touch of other colour.

Busy Lizzie, see **IMPATIENS SULTANII**

CALATHEA ORNATA Eight inch, spear-like leaves dark green striped pink or white and with purple undersides, borne on long stems. Keep warm and humid, out of direct sun. A striking temporary plant difficult to keep for long but attractive in a group, preferably plunged. *C. zebrina* has slightly different colouring and a more velvety texture.

Canary island ivy, see **HEDERA CANARIENSIS**
Cast iron plant, see **ASPIDISTRA ELATIOR**
Chestnut vine, see **TETRASTIGMA VOINIERIANUM**

Chinese evergreen, see **AGLAONEMA COMMUTATUM**

CHLOROPHYTUM COMOSUM VARIEGATUM (Spider plant) Long, grass-like leaves, striped green and white, arching from a central point and long stems bearing baby plants at their tips. An easy and rewarding plant, growing under almost all conditions. Best placed high in a room to allow the long stems with their interesting young plants to hang downwards.

Christmas cactus, see **ZYGOCACTUS TRUNCATUS**

CHRYSANTHEMUM Many year-round chrysanthemums are now inexpensive and available in pots. A good, easy flowering plant in many colours that does well as a colourful specimen or colour-blended in a group. Normal room conditions suit.

CINERARIA CRUENTIS A familiar little plant with many colours of daisy-like flowers. Normally fairly easy in the home for short periods, but inclined to be a "dirty" plant, attracting greenfly, so spray with systemic insecticide at the first sign of pests. Best grouped together in several colours.

CISSUS ANTARCTICA (Kangaroo vine) A good green climber that will live for years in the home and cover an entire wall with support. Normal home conditions suit it, with plenty of water in spring and summer, less in winter. Feed fortnightly to obtain good growth. Useful as a screen, a wall covering or as a pillar.

CODIAEUM VARIEGATUM PICTUM (Croton) An attractive plant with shining leaves blotched with green, gold, red, white. Only the newest varieties are possible indoors for long periods. Keep warm and humid, preferably spraying daily. Particularly good for mixing in plant groups.

COLEUS Gorgeous multicoloured hybrids with many forms, patterns and colours. Keep warm and well watered. Pick off all the little insignificant flowers as they appear. Splendid alone when a good, large specimen. Smaller samples do well bringing colour to groups of green plants.

COLUMNEA BANKSII A pretty trailer with many dark green leaves from which appear many vivid tubular scarlet flowers. *C. microphylla* is similar but with smaller

Coleus
Of all the foliage plants the coleus is one of the most attractive for its wide range of colours.

Forsythia
Sprays of this early-flowering shrub are excellent for early spring cut-flower arrangements.

Cineraria (front right) and hydrangea (rear left)

leaves. As flowers appear in winter give as much light as possible, even direct sunlight. Keep warm and moderately watered. Best on a tall stand as a specimen, the green and scarlet trails making a brilliant spectacle.

CORDYLINE TERMINALIS (Flaming dragon tree) Usually sold as *Dracaena terminalis*. Long, vivid, shining, spear-shaped leaves in green and red. Keep

Dieffenbachia (Dumb cane)

warm and moist and in good light. Best as a specimen plant when in good condition, but when lower leaves brown and fall disguise this by placing among other plants in a group.

Crab cactus, see **ZYGOCACTUS TRUNCATUS**

Croton, see **CODIAEUM VARIEGATUM PICTUM**

Crown of thorns, see **EUPHORBIA BOJERI**

CRYPTANTHUS ACAULIS (Earth star) Just one of several cryptanthuses, useful bromeliads, with long leaves growing in a rosette, many coloured in the different varieties. Water lightly, keep in good light. Most are earth hugging plants and are most striking when grown wired or nailed to cork bark, driftwood or a log.

CYCLAMEN Corm grown flowers, sometimes with lovely foliage, pink, white, red, purple or sometimes flecked. Keep in cool conditions in good light and make sure the soil is always uniformly moist. Remove all fading flowers by plucking the entire stem straight from the corm. Good, large specimens best displayed alone, younger or smaller plants look well in groups together, but not with mixed plants.

CYPERUS ALTERNIFOLIUS GRACILIS (Galingale) A grass-like bog plant growing on tall stems, foliage branching out like umbrella ribs with a tiny tuft of insignificant flowers on top. Must have plenty of water at all times. Keep warm. Useful in groups as a contrast in shape.

Daffodil, see **NARCISSUS**

DIEFFENBACHIA PICTA (Dumb cane) A striking, attractive and useful plant with large green leaves speckled and blotched with cream and white. *D. amoena* is similar but with more regular stripes. Keep warm, well watered, out of direct sun. Highly poisonous plants, no part of the plant or its sap should be allowed to enter the mouth as it causes intense pain with swelling leading to temporary dumbness.

DIZYGOTHECA ELEGANTISSIMA A tree-like plant with central stem from which grow short stems bearing long, slender, toothed leaves. Elegant and striking, requiring warmth and much humidity. Excellent as a specimen and when lower leaves drop this fact can be concealed by placing it in a group, where its unusual leaf shape adds interest.

DRACAENA SANDERIANA Long glossy green leaves white margined. Different are *D. godseffiana, D. goldieana* and *D. marginata.* All are attractive and useful, demanding warm and humid conditions out of sun. Use as specimen or in groups depending on condition.

Dumb cane, see **DIEFFENBACHIA PICTA**

Earth star, see **CRYPTANTHUS ACAULIS**

ERICA GRACILIS (Heather) One of two potted heathers seen mainly at Christmas. The other is *E.*

Hedera
(Ivy)

Fittonia
(Snake skin plant)

hyemalis. Both are attractive but short lived. Spray daily with clean rain water and use rain water also for daily watering, for they are lime haters and must never be allowed to dry out. Best as specimens.

EUPHORBIA BOJERI (Crown of thorns) So called because of the vicious spines and the tiny, blood red flowers. A succulent, so place in direct sun, water moderately in spring and summer but rarely in winter. Because of thorns must be kept as a specimen plant. Another of the same family is *Euphorbia pulcherrima,* the poinsettia, with vivid scarlet, white or pink bracts at the top of the plant. Always keep warm and well watered in plenty of strong light but not direct sun. They dislike temperature changes. Good plants as specimens but useful in a group when the lower leaves have fallen.

FATSHEDERA LIZEI A cross between a fatsia and a hedera, with large palmate leaves growing from a main stem. Easy and tolerant, living well under normal room conditions. Will grow to 10 feet or more. A fine screening or columnar plant, but small specimens look well grouped. A variegated form is available.

FICUS ELASTICA DECORA (Rubber plant) A familiar house plant and a member of the useful fig family which provides several other good plants for the home. It is also available in variegated form. Plenty of water in spring and summer but little in winter. Too much or too little water will cause leaves to turn yellow and fall. Keep leaves clean. Large plants can only be used as specimens or in a large group with smaller plants at the base.

FITTONIA ARGYRONEURA (Snake skin plant) A small, but very beautiful plant with large green leaves delicately veined with silver. Difficult but worthwhile, demanding much humidity, warmth and a shady place in the home. So lovely that it must be kept as a specimen.

Flaming dragon tree, see **CORDYLINE TERMINALIS**

Flamingo flower, see **ANTHURIUM ANDREANUM**

Galingale, see **CYPERUS ALTERNIFOLIUS GRACILIS**

Geranium, see **PELARGONIUM**

Goldfish plant, see **HYPOCYRTA GLABRA**

Goose foot plant, see **SYNGONIUM PODOPHYLLUM**
Grape ivy, see **RHOICISSUS RHOMBOIDEA**
Greek vase plant, see **AECHMEA RHODOCYANEA**
Heather, see **ERICA GRACILIS**

HEDERA CANARIENSIS (Canary Island ivy) One of many ivies which are so useful, tolerant and decorative as house plants. This one is a trailer or climber with gold and green leaves. All the hederas are comparatively easy to grow and extremely long lasting. They tolerate normal room conditions well. They can be used as climbers, trailers or pillars, as a screen or covering.

HELXINE SOLEIROLII (Baby's tears) A little creeping plant with tiny bright green leaves borne on black, wiry stems, which spreads to cover pot and almost anything around it if given plenty of water at all times and kept out of hot sun. A good plant to grow in an open group where it can spread and carpet neighbouring pots and soil.

HYACINTH Too familiar to require description, this bulb flower can be grown in the home in a special hyacinth glass, in soil or in pebbles. Pre-cooled bulbs allow flowers as early as Christmas.

HYPOCYRTA GLABRA (Goldfish plant) A little plant with small green leaves and bright orange-red flowers that give it its popular name. Easy to grow in the home. Too small as a specimen, but excellent grouped, where it lightens other green plants.

IMPATIENS SULTANII (Busy Lizzie) A familiar and useful flowering plant which has many forms and colours. Keep soil always moist and feed regularly when in bloom. Under correct care and good conditions will make a large plant. Cuttings root easily in soil or just in water. Either a specimen or in groups.

KALANCHOE A succulent with many forms and varieties, increasingly popular as new forms are bred. Attractive flowers and thick, fleshy foliage, sometimes coloured. Easy to keep indoors with normal treatment and usually flowering in winter. Excellent to give colour in groups or as a small specimen for the coffee table or sideboard.

Kangaroo vine, see **CISSUS ANTARCTICA**
Maidenhair fern, see **ADIANTUM CUNEATUM**

MARANTA MAKOYANA (Peacock plant) A lovely plant with beautiful leaves in tones of green with pink and brown markings. Sometimes difficult, but given right conditions will live and flourish for many months. Keep warm and humid, away from draughts and direct sun. A fine plant for bottle gardens.

MONSTERA DELICIOSA (Swiss cheese plant) The large, green leaves of this climber are slashed with holes, which is the reason for its popular name. It will grow very large, at least 20–30 feet in length, around the top of a room. Keep in a shady spot, roots uniformly moist, and never move it from its first home as it likes to

Maranta (Peacock plant)

stay put. Young specimens can be used in groups but the older and larger they are the more slashed and holed the leaves become, hence the more interesting.

Mother-in-law's tongue, see **SANSEVIERIA TRIFASCIATA LAURENTII**

Mother of thousands, see **SAXIFRAGA STOLONIFERA**

NARCISSUS (Daffodil) Many daffodils can be grown in the home but only a few force well for early bloom. They can be grown in soil, bulb fibre or in pebbles.

NEOREGELIA CAROLINAE TRICOLOR Another useful bromeliad with strap like leaves growing from a central "vase" which should be kept topped up with water at all times. The foot long, narrow, saw-toothed leaves are green with a central white stripe except when the plant is about to produce its insignificant flowers from the centre of the rosette. The centre

Nidularium

then turns a soft pink which gradually deepens until it is a fiery scarlet. Use mainly as a specimen plant and place low in the room so the centre can be seen.

NIDULARIUM MARECHATI Still another bromeliad, this time with somewhat wider, fleshier leaves, a solid dark green. These too blush to a fiery scarlet when the flower is produced. Treatment and use are much the same as with the neoregelia and indeed most other members of the bromeliad family.

Norfolk Island pine, see **ARAUCARIA EXCELSA**

Palette plant, see **ANTHURIUM SCHERZERIANUM**

PANDANUS SANDERI (Screw pine) A grass-like plant with large green and gold leaves which will grow to about 2 feet. Water freely in summer, sparsely in winter, keep warm and humid. Best grown in groups, where its lighter colouring and sword-like leaves lighten a dark green mass.

Parlour palm, see **ASPIDISTRA ELATIOR**

Peacock plant, see **MARANTA MAKOYANA**

PELARGONIUM (Geranium) A gay and familiar plant of many forms and colours. Can be grown for long periods in the home, and with proper care will flower almost the year through. Keep in a light position, even in full sun, and water heavily in summer and still occasionally in winter. Pick off all dead flowers and feed regularly for good flower production.

PEPEROMIA CAPERATA A small plant with dark, grey-green leaves, crinkled and waved and bearing tall rat-tail flowers. Also available in variegated form. Keep warm and humid, light and only just moist, summer and winter. *P. magnoliaefolia variegata* has larger, fleshier, glossier leaves of green and gold. Both are too small to be used as specimens except for special positions.

PHILODENDRON SCANDENS Probably the most popular example of this very large family of aroids, many of which give us excellent and tolerant house plants. All are climbers in their native tropical America and all can make magnificent and dramatic decorations for the home. Several will grow and climb up a piece of bark or a moss covered cane. Keep generally moist and warm, with less water in winter. Most will grow in shade. First class plants for screens.

Piggy tail plant, see **ANTHURIUM SCHERZERIANUM**

PLATYCERIUM BIFURCATUM (Stag's horn fern) A fleshy leaved fern with grey-green leaves closely resembling a stag's horns in shape. Best grown on a block of wood and suspended high in a room, where the fronds can hang attractively. Water by plunging the entire plant in a bucket of water and allowing it to drain before replacing in position. Allow to dry out almost completely between waterings.

PLECTRANTHUS FRUTICOSUS An engaging climber and trailer with shining green leaves on long trails. Easy and tolerant, will grow in sun or shade. Give plenty of water in summer and a regular feed, cutting down on both when the days grow colder and shorter. Hang high on a wall for the trails to curve downwards attractively.

Poinsettia, see **EUPHORBIA PULCHERRIMA**

PRIMULA Several forms available, from the wild *P. vulgaris* to the more cultivated *P. obconica*. They grow well indoors for comparatively short spells and are useful mainly as harbingers of spring and dispellers of winter gloom. Give plenty of water, some warmth, plenty of light and protection from all draughts and fumes. Best as tiny and endearing specimen plants.

RHOICISSUS RHOMBOIDEA (Grape ivy) An easily grown climber, tolerant of home conditions, that will cover an entire wall or form a dense screen. Water freely most of the year so long as it is kept warm. Give a light position out of direct sunlight. Feed regularly to get good continuous growth, which will need supporting by canes or string.

Rubber plant, see **FICUS ELASTICA**

Saffron spike, see **APHELANDRA SQUARROSA LOUISAE**

SAINTPAULIA IONANTHA (African violet) An endearing little plant with hairy leaves which with correct treatment will bear masses of little violet-like flowers, single or double, white, pink, purple, blue or mauve. Impossible to keep indoors with any domestic gas in the atmosphere and difficult for many people because of atmospheric pollution. Keep warm, moist, shaded and in steady temperatures. Good plants can act as speci-

Primula

Sansevieria (Mother-in-law's tongue)

mens, but usually they are better in groups together with several different kinds and colours.

SANSEVIERIA TRIFASCIATA LAURENTII (Mother-in-law's tongue) The long, sharp, sword-like leaves are the somewhat obvious origin of the popular name. They are a mottled green with a golden stripe along the edges. This is an easy and tolerant plant with an almost succulent-like acceptance of dry conditions. It will grow to three feet or more. Water regularly in summer but never let it get too wet and keep almost dry in winter. A fine plant with a dozen or more spikes makes a good specimen plant, but this is sometimes too much for a group, where smaller examples give good contrast of shape and form. A good plant for giving the appearance of added height to a room.

SAXIFRAGA STOLONIFERA (Aaron's beard; mother of thousands) Round, strawberry-like leaves, hairy and reddish green. It produces many fine, hair-like runners bearing baby plants at the tips. For this reason grow it high on a wall or on a stand so that these can hang. Water freely in summer, sparingly in winter. Keep cool and shaded.

SCINDAPSUS AUREUS A climber with heart-shaped leaves of green flecked and marbled with gold. It requires good light in order to keep its leaf colour but it must never have direct sunlight or they will burn. Keep slightly on the dry side, but on hot days spray with clean water. Merges and contrasts well with *Philodendron scandens* which it so much resembles. A good screen and columnar plant.

Screw pine, see **PANDANUS SANDERI**
Shrimp plant, see **BELOPERONE GUTTATA**
Snake skin plant, see **FITTONIA ARGYRONEURA**

SOLANUM CAPSICASTRUM (Winter cherry) A little plant with scarlet or orange berries frequently seen in stores and markets at Christmas. It seldom lasts long but makes an attractive seasonal decoration. Keep cool and in a draught-free, well-lit spot. Give an occasional spray with tepid water. Gives a festive air to an all green arrangement.

SPATHIPHYLLUM WALLISII A useful plant with shining green spear-shaped leaves and large, white,

Spathiphyllum

arum lily-like flowers. These flowers are actually a white spathe surrounding a yellow-green spadix. The spathiphyllum tolerates unusually dark conditions and because the white flowers shine out here this makes it a good plant for a dark corner or a hallway. Give plenty of water and a regular feed to keep the flowers bright and long lasting.

Spider plant, see **CHLOROPHYTUM COMOSUM VARIEGATUM**

Stag's horn fern, see **PLATYCERIUM BIFURCATUM**

Swiss cheese plant, see **MONSTERA DELICIOSA**

SYNGONIUM PODOPHYLLUM (Goosefoot plant) The leaf shape dictates the popular name of this plant, which though tolerant of poor conditions really shines at its best when looked after carefully. Warmth, light shade, plenty of water in summer and very little in winter are its main requirements. This is a plant for grouping, where the leaf shape contrasts well.

TETRASTIGMA VOINIERIANUM (Chestnut vine) This is a real monster, to be grown only where there

Tradescantia
(Wandering Jew)

is plenty of room. It grows during winter and given warm conditions it will grow an inch a day, pushing its chestnut tree-shaped leaves up to the ceiling. Young growth is a silver green, slightly downy, changing to a darker and sturdier green. It likes plenty of water at all times and regular feeding while it grows. In summer it hardly moves. A special plant for a special situation.

TRADESCANTIA FLUMINENSIS (Wandering Jew, Wandering sailor) Perhaps the most frequently seen of all house plants, available in silver and golden forms while tinges of violet can be induced in good light. Tradescantias are seldom grown as well as they should be, generally because they are allowed to grow too old. Longer shoots should be nipped off and re-potted in the same pot to make thicker growth. Give plenty of water in summer, less in winter and an occasional feed. Keep in good light. A good plant for a high spot where the trails can hang down or in a group where they can tumble over and soften the edge of the container.

VRIESIA FENESTRALIS Still another splendid bromeliad. The rosette of narrow, strap-like leaves spreads out from the centre to make a plant some two feet across. These leaves are beautifully and delicately marked with dark and light green, brown and mauve. Keep in light shade and top up central "vase" instead of watering the soil. A warm situation preferred. Because of the fascination of the leaf colouring this should be a specimen plant capable of close inspection. *Vriesia hieroglyphica* has dark green leaves marked with purple-black.

Wandering Jew, Wandering sailor, see **TRADESCANTIA FLUMINENSIS**

Winter cherry, see **SOLANUM CAPSICASTRUM**

Zebra plant, see **APHELANDRA SQUARROSA LOUISAE**

ZEBRINA PENDULA Like tradescantia but with slightly larger, fleshier leaves more vividly coloured, frequently with an almost metallic silver sheen. Slower growing than tradescantia, so not so necessary to cut it back so frequently, but treatment and use much the same.

ZYGOCACTUS TRUNCATUS (Christmas cactus, Crab cactus) The first common name is because it frequently flowers at about Christmas time and the second because the fleshy stems have a similar appearance to crab claws. The flowers are large, spectacular and brilliant, usually scarlet, pink or white. Give plenty of light, even direct sunlight when not in bloom. Water well in summer and when in bloom, but when the flowers have finished allow to dry out almost completely. A well flowered plant is good enough to be treated as a specimen, otherwise the plant mixes well in a group.

A still-life of gourds in a wicker basket.

A truly magnificent display of gladioli.

Everlasting flowers (Helichrysum)
In addition to their use in cut-flower arrangements some species can be grown in pots indoors.

7 POT-ET-FLEUR

Most of our house plants are grown for their foliage, which, though interesting and frequently lovely in shape, colour and texture, does not make the same impact of flowers. There is no reason why we should not use both together, so that one complements the other and we thereby get the most of both worlds. The name given to this type of arrangement is pot-et-fleur, descriptive though in dubious French and coined after a competition organised by my wife through the columns of a national newspaper some years ago.

Pot-et-fleur opens tremendous opportunities for the home decorator, but though it sounds simple it is not actually as easy as it seems. The decorator must have a considerable knowledge of both plants and flowers, an almost instinctive feeling of which plants and which flowers will mingle attractively, as well as a deep experience of shape, colour, texture and habit of growth of the plants to be used. Sheer technical skill in handling and arranging flowers and plants is also required.

Yet all pot-et-fleur need not be complex. One of the simplest examples concerns bulb flowers grown for winter decoration in the home. We have all at one time or another forced hyacinths into early bloom by planting them in a bowl, keeping them cool and dark and then

Mixed arrangement of cut hyacinths, tradescantia and cryptanthus

6

bringing them into our living rooms when roots are formed and the flowers are about to appear. But there is still some time to wait before the flowers grow and open and in this interim period the planted bowl can appear somewhat dull and uninteresting. To make a pot-et-fleur arrangement in this case it is possible to plant the bulbs around the circumference of a large bowl in the normal manner and to place in the centre an empty flower pot. When the bowl is brought into the living room the empty pot is removed and replaced with a pot in which a house plant is growing.

The house plant then occupies the place of interest while the bulbs gradually grow and unfold their flowers. A knowledge of plants and the type of growth they make is necessary in choosing the right plant for this empty space. The plant must be comparatively small and it must be low growing. It must not cast dense shade over the growing bulbs. It must be sufficiently colourful and interesting to occupy its important position for a brief period, yet not so dominant that it takes precedence over the hyacinth flowers when they appear, and its colour or colours must harmonise attractively with these flowers. The answer will probably be a tradescantia, zebrina, small ivy, a little peperomia or some such comparatively neutral yet interesting plant capable of accepting the limelight before the emergence of the flowers yet capable too of retiring into the background when they are in their full glory.

A further point for consideration concerns the care of both plants and flowers. In this case the flowers are growing and are not cut, so both the bulbs and the potted plant require moisture at their roots.

But this would be impossible if cut flowers were to be used with the hyacinth bulbs instead of the growing plant. On the other hand, instead of placing a potted plant in the centre of the burgeoning bowl of bulbs, it would be quite possible to insert in the vacant space a small, low container and arrange some flowers in this. But as these flowers would be unlikely to look well with the opening hyacinths, a plant is used instead.

If we go to the other extreme and consider using a plant of considerable stature and dignity, we have to look rather more closely at both our choices and our tech-

Philodendron,
ivy and
arums in a
copper saucepan

Mixed arrangement of begonia, seed pots, dracaena, driftwood and lilies

niques. Let us say that we have a ten foot *Monstera deliciosa* growing in the hallway in a large, Victorian decorated slop pail. For a special occasion, a party or a reception, we wish to add further interest and glamour to this already large and decorative plant. The monstera is an aroid, so arum lilies would be a particularly apposite choice, having a natural affinity. They also have long, smooth, naked stems, similar to the stems of the monstera. They are not, in fact, too unlike the flowers of the monstera, though few of us have an opportunity in this country to grow a plant to its flowering stage.

But how are we to use cut stems of arum lilies with a tall plant of this nature? It is possible to buy from florist sundriesmen and some general stores green painted metal cones from four or five inches to a foot or more in length. One or two of these, tied or taped behind a stem of the monstera can be filled with water and used as a receptacle for the arum stems. The flowers can be propped or held by the monstera leaves so that they appear dramatically, gleaming white or yellow against the large, green, slashed and holed leaves.

The flowers will last a considerable time in their water-filled cone holders and when they begin to fade they can easily be removed and replaced or the cones can be untied to leave the plant unharmed, undamaged and

Mixed arrangement of cut hyacinths, tradescantia and African violets

standing alone again as a decorative feature on its own. The cones can, of course, be used over and over again and in certain circumstances it is even possible to make your own flower cones using tablet tubes, test tubes, or even a child's balloon, filled with water, the stem or stems inserted and then tied securely in place.

Perhaps the most important point of pot-et-fleur, then, is that whereas the plant or plants concerned can live for many months, any flowers used will have a much more temporary life, but they can be replaced at any time with flowers of the same kind or with different flowers with different colours. The plants become a background, a frame for the flowers.

Yet although we cannot expect cut flowers to be as long lasting as potted plants, we can at least ensure that they last as long as possible and it is necessary that they be given a good, long, deep drink before being arranged in their positions. Tulips, for example, with their long, straight stems and their sculptured appearance are excellent with many plants, particularly climbers, but are sometimes apt to bend and snake their stems if arranged too quickly after being bought or cut from the garden. Wrap them firmly in a sheet of newspaper and stand them like this in a bucket of water which reaches right up to the flower heads. Left overnight, or for several hours in a cool, dark place, they will become strong and turgid and their life will be extended by as many as three or four days.

Orchids are exceptionally long lasting and again have the clean lines that are so helpful in pot-et-fleur. Many are imported today and prices are not high when it is realised that they will last indoors for as long as six weeks. Cymbidiums are probably best and long sprays can be bought which can be "planted" in a cone or tablet tube of water at the base, for example, of a billbergia or a *Philodendron imbe,* to appear to grow up through the leaves and even appear to be a part of the plant.

Equally long lasting are fruits. These vary enormously according to variety and can range from normal domestic fruits such as gleaming, polished apples to sprays of wild berries from the hedgerow. Individual fruits such as apples cannot, of course, be kept in water unless a spray of brilliantly coloured crab apples or some of the smaller cider apples are used, in which case the woody stem end can be placed in water in a hidden receptacle.

To get the most brilliant effect, long lasting and trouble free, use fruit as the major part of your arrangement and plants as the minor decoration. For example, pile a bowl or comport with a mixture of normal edible fruits, such as apples, bananas and oranges. In the centre of this place a cryptanthus or two, pots enveloped in a polythene bag for cleanliness and safety in watering. The fruit can be replaced as it is consumed and the plants will live for many months, which means that you can have a continuous, attractive and labour saving decoration in the home throughout the winter at minimum cost.

Another ideal winter arrangement, particularly pleasing for the centre of the dining table can be made up by placing in the centre of the fruit bowl a small round container holding a pinholder and filled with water. Arrange on the pinholder just three or four stems of daffodils and perhaps some crinkled, acid green stem ends of forced rhubarb. Around and between these place the fruits that will end the meal: apples, bananas, oranges and a bunch of fat green grapes hanging down to soften the edge of the container. This makes a useful, made-in-a-moment decoration when you are entertaining and provides, too, an amusing talking point.

Here the colours all blend beautifully and it is happily the case that it is always possible to choose plants and flowers that blend prettily. A vivid purple, red and silver Begonia rex, for example, can be used with the similarly coloured but more pointed leaves of *Cordyline terminalis,* their pots one behind another so that the cordyline towers above the begonia. A short and slim tablet tube hidden by the pots will hold a single rose red tulip, its petals opened to display all its colour and a bunch of purple grapes can complete the ensemble and add to the rich and royal colours.

Look for similarity of shapes as well as colours. The tuft at the top of a pineapple is very like the tuft at the top of a stem of fritillarias; the pointed flowers of arums and spathiphyllum go well with the spear-shaped leaves of many philodendrons; tulips blend happily with many aroids; the autumn tints and the starry shapes of chrysanthemums combine with the maranta or zebra plant.

Although it is usually easier to arrange your plants in their pots and fix the flowers in an added or accessory container of some type, occasionally it may be better to reverse the process, particularly where plant pots may be too large for your decoration or where there is the possibility that soil may fall or watering can cause damage. In this case either slip the entire plant pot inside a polythene bag and seal the top with a rubber band, or knock the plant from its pot and slip the root ball inside a bag. If the top of the bag is sealed as suggested with a rubber band then it helps to retain moisture and the root ball will require watering at much less frequent intervals. This technique is particularly useful when you wish your plants to remain in position for some time without having to re-arrange them for watering. When you have finished with the decoration make sure that the plant is re-potted securely so that it continues to give decorative value in the home.

Generally speaking the foliage of house plants is dominant in a pot-et-fleur arrangement. This imposes on us certain rules of taste and proportion which we should follow in order to obtain the most pleasing results. Flowers, for example, should be bold and dramatic, yet they should be subservient to the overall pattern and theme dictated by the plant or plants employed. Flower foliage should be minimal unless by some happy chance or clever choice it continues the general shape of the plant foliage. Large flowers should be used in preference to small, which can look merely fussy. Yet sometimes small flowers can be bunched or posied to give the effect of a single large bloom and they can also be used with effect to give the impression of carpeting the ground at the base of a larger plant.

Because the foliage of the plants used in pot-et-fleur is usually dominant, this gives us the advantage that containers for cut flowers can easily be hidden and that flower stems can be fixed in position with transparent adhesive tape or by green twine without these artifices being apparent. So there is no need to be hesitant in the creation of outsize, unusual or even bizarre decorations which fulfill the function of decorating the home.

Although pot-et-fleur is an art particularly useful during the winter months as it brings extra colour into the home without extravagant expenditure, it can be a year-round hobby also. With skill and taste it can bring a new insight into the leaf shape, the colour and the habit of growth of a plant which otherwise might be passed over without a second glance.

Mixed arrangement of carrot flower, oats, briony, viburnum and santolina

8 ACCESSORIES AND DRIED FLOWERS

Flowers and plants are so beautiful and so universally loved that it is sometimes difficult to understand why they should be complemented by accessories such as driftwood, shells, stones and other decorative additions. Yet when one considers for a moment the purpose of a flower or plant arrangement in the home one can see that anything that adds to the total decorative effect is not only permissible but almost obligatory, for if a thing is worth doing at all it is best to do it as well as possible.

Driftwood is, of course, a natural material, usually, as its name implies, a piece of wood which has been cleaned, smoothed and even polished through long immersion in sea, river or lake. It can also consist of gnarled and twisted roots, burnt stems of gorse, coils of ivy. Today it can be semi-artificial, by which I mean that attractively shaped stems are now dried, sand-blasted and smoothed until they have the colour and the patina of the natural product. There has even been an attempt to introduce plastic driftwood to the flower arranger,

An attractive display of arum lilies and sprays of salix

Tulips and driftwood in a ceramic container

though happily perhaps with little lasting effect. The natural product is selected mainly for its shape, though its bleached and neutral colour must also be taken into account. Long immersion in water and the drying effects of sun and wind mean that all insect life is killed and the pieces are safe to bring into the home.

It takes a good eye for line to choose an effective piece of driftwood and the clever arranger will see the possibilities in a tangle of stems that carries no meaning for the uninitiated. A lovely shape can be cut from a larger piece or sometimes two or more pieces will be used together, the joints hidden by the normal artifices of flower arrangement. Driftwood is generally used to give line, shape and flow to an arrangement of flowers or plants and the dedicated arranger will have a collection of many pieces from which to choose. They last almost for ever unless broken or cut for some special design and can be used again and again, sometimes facing one way or another, sometimes used vertically or horizontally, one way up or the other.

Any attractively shaped piece of natural wood can be bleached and smoothed quite easily and if found it is well to put the treasure aside for treatment. Normally all bark should be removed to reveal the clean inner surface. This can then be immersed for some days in a solution of ordinary household bleach before being removed and left to dry in the sun. Careful trimming to shape and filing or sandpapering ragged or snagged edges or corners helps to give the finished product a groomed and elegant appearance.

Another product of the seashore frequently used to good effect in flower and plant arrangement is shells. These can vary enormously in shape, size, colour and texture and it is because of their qualities in these lines that they find their function in this decorative art. They have, in fact, a natural affinity with flower arrangement because of their connection with water. All fresh cut flowers must be arranged in water and an attractive shell or group of shells in or near the water can add to the general effect. Most shells only reveal their true colours

Striking arrangement of achillea and water grass

when under water, becoming less vivid and losing their patina when dry. A little strand of creamy-grey periwinkle shells, for example, becomes a bright and shining yellow when water is added and is obviously delightful spread under the springtime promise of yellow daffodils.

Some shells are large enough to act as complete containers, either for flowers or for plants. If they are collected or bought with care and stored safely they last almost for ever. Unusual shells, both in colour and in shape are more frequently to be bought than found on the seashore unless you are fortunate enough to visit strange and exotic lands. Several specialists maintain large stocks of unusual shells at prices which are modest when it is understood how long they will last and the multifarious purposes to which they can be put.

Less immediately obvious in their decorative value are stones, which can vary just as widely as shells. They can vary from the rough and craggy to the smooth, polished and almost gem-like. They should either be weathered or smooth, for there should be no disintegration if they are placed in or under water. Some sandstones and limestones tend to crumble and soften and these should be avoided unless they are so suited for some particular arrangement that their use cannot aesthetically be avoided.

Some tropical fish and aquaria dealers stock stones which not only remain solid under water but which actually gain in colour through being submerged. They also carry supplies of raw glass in rock-like lumps, plain or coloured, and this can be both useful and long lived in flower arrangements.

Although the use of accessories such as those mentioned here is frequently for their added colour, texture or form, they can also be highly purposeful in the mechanics of flower and plant arrangement. Where a tall group of tulips, for example, rises impaled on a pinholder in the centre of a round glass bowl, shells, stones, driftwood carry out a useful as well as a decorative purpose in hiding the unattractive pinholder and making the decoration more pleasing. In arranging all flowers some means of holding them in position is necessary and this is almost always unpleasing in appearance, so accessories can help us here, although we should not forget

Chincherinchees arrayed against a coral fan

that in most cases it is also possible to hide the mechanics of arrangement by means of an artfully placed leaf or a curving stem.

A further accessory that rests on the borderline and can sometimes be used as a decorative material is various forms of fungi. Mushrooms and toadstools can sometimes be used to decorative effect, but they are comparatively short lived and always delicate to handle, but other forms of fungi can sometimes be both very large and very firm in texture. Some bracket fungi found growing on trees are so large that they can actually be used as containers for plants and if carefully dried will last for many months. Colours generally fade as they dry, becoming a pleasant and inoffensive tan or grey, suitable for mixing with almost all flowers or plants.

Nearly all plant material will dry, in fact, and can provide us with natural decorative shapes and textures which are long lasting and will neither fade nor wilt under the warm and dry conditions of our homes. But as most plants lose their decorative effect when dried it is necessary to learn a little about drying and treating techniques and to recognise which plants are most suited to this kind of treatment.

True everlastings or perpetuelles are easy to grow in your own garden. Treat them as half-hardy annuals, sow seeds in greenhouse or in frames or cloches in March and set the new plants outdoors in May or June. Perhaps the best known of the perpetuelles is the helichrysum or straw daisy, but there are also the helipterums or acrocliniums, statice or limoniums, anaphalis, ammobiums and catananches. All of these are easy to grow at home and all can easily be bought in normal florist shops.

Pick helichrysums as soon as the blooms are ready and of a good, fat size. Do not try to save the stems, but get the flowers only and dry them on a wire netting shelf which will allow air to pass all around and under them. Make sure that they are absolutely dry before you begin to store them.

The pink or white helipterums or acrocliniums are smaller and more endearing than the helichrysums, but just as useful. Treat them in much the same way, picking, without stems, as they mature, and drying them on a shelf which will allow air to circulate all around them.

These may be collected singly or in bunches, in which case all the blooms in a bunch may not have matured equally. Yet if some are ready it is worth while picking the bunch in order to have a number of smaller buds to use. The most popular type is *Helipterum roseum*, but smaller flowers will be found on *H. manglesii.*

The sea lavender is still popularly known as statice although it is botanically limonium. There are several of these: *L. sinuatum* can be blue, white, cream and a soft peach colour. *L. suworowii* is known as 'candlewick statice', a soft lilac-pink and so naturally drooping in habit that when collected it is helpful to hang it head down to allow the blooms to dry in this position. There are also *L. latifolium*, lavender blue and similar to gypsophyla, two to three feet tall and branching, and *L. incana*, with white flowers, shorter and stockier.

The so-called 'pearly everlasting' is anaphalis, freely flowered and easy to dry. *A. triplinervis* is the best, but there is also *A. margaritacaea*. Wait until these are quite mature before cutting the stems and hanging them up head downward to dry.

Only the largest of the ammobiums, *A. alatum*, is worth growing in this country. These, the everlasting sand flowers, should be watched carefully and cut just before they mature, being hung up in a dry cool spot to dry and mature before use.

The catananche, particularly the blue *C. caerulea,* is good for drying and with its slightly different shape makes a worthwhile perpetuelle. Gather it just before it matures to capture the lovely blue and hang head downwards in an airy but dark spot.

So like clover in appearance that it has been called Spanish clover is the globe amaranth, globe clover or gomphrena. *G. globosa* comes in purple, red or white; *G. carnea* in flesh pink and *G. aurea superba* in yellow. All are good dryers but need a little special attention and a higher temperature than the others, needing a greenhouse to bring them to maturity.

And finally in this easy list of grow-it-yourself flowers is the xeranthemum, a white or purple daisy which is easy to grow but not so easy to obtain, only a few seedsmen listing the several varieties in their catalogues.

The few flowers listed above are grown mainly as

dried materials and apart from unusually inclement conditions can be relied upon to give useful blooms in most years. There are a considerable number of other flowers which can be dried but which serve mainly as decoration in the garden. All lose their colour somewhat when dried and all are subject to weather and general climatic conditions when being dried, so that in some years they will be splendid, full of colour and crisp, clean and easy to use, while in a wet season they may develop moulds, lose their colour or even fail miserably when put in the shed or airing cupboard. It is usually best to allow them all to dry slowly and carefully, preferably in a shed or outhouse where there is plenty of air to circulate about them and no sun to dry them out too quickly.

The following brief list includes the majority of the flowers that dry easily under normal conditions, keep some semblance of their colour and are comparatively easy to handle once they have dried.

Achilleas dry on their own stems, which are strong and sturdy, not even requiring to be hung head downward. Cut *A. filipendulina* when the flowers are young

Mixed arrangement of gomphrena lonas, briza, ammobium, etc.

Narcissus

Perhaps the most beautiful of all the spring flowers. They are equally attractive in cut-flower arrangements or when grown individually in pots.

Peonies

The richly coloured large blooms of these flowers make striking backgrounds for cut-flower arrangements.

but bright in colour and stand them heads up in a dry vase for the flowers to dry. It is best to strip the stems of leaves, which appear somewhat unattractive when dried, but even this is not obligatory.

Orange, red or crimson cockscombs, *Celosia plumosa*, dry well. Gather them just before they mature, strip all foliage, tie in small bunches and hang head downwards to dry.

Delphiniums, particularly the belladonna types, with their characteristic blue, are always useful, though the colour does fade somewhat in the drying process. Strip leaves and hang head downwards in small bunches, preferably in a slightly warmer atmosphere such as the airing cupboard.

Globe thistles, echinops, can be cut on their stems which will dry strong and sturdy. Buddleia spikes will keep their colour and their shape and the perennial gypsophila, dainty but sturdy, is useful as a filler. Young blooms of some heathers last a long time and keep their colour well.

Hydrangeas are wonderful dried flowers if they are

Mixed display of hydrangeas (preserved), beech leaves, delphiniums and chrysanthemums

7

Striking display of barley, laurel leaves, magnolia leaves, pine cones, gourds, tulip and poppy heads grouped on a Victorian stand

collected and treated with understanding. The colourful bracts must be allowed to dry out and become almost papery on the plant before they are picked. The actual flowers are in the centres of these bracts, quite insignificant, but they must be allowed to die away before the bracts are ready for collecting. They then need no additional treatment.

Lavender flowers should be picked before they are really mature, or they will drop and make a nuisance of themselves.

Pussy willow dries easily and can be used to give a breath of simulated spring even while winter is gathering strength to give of its worst. Merely cut the stems and allow them to dry. Choose slightly immature stems. These keep their colour and appearance remarkably well and have an additional bonus in that they hold curves well. When drying pussy willow it is helpful to save a few stems and curve them gently in the hands. Some stems can be curved into a complete circle and tied in this position. They can then be weighted down under water over night and when the tie is removed they will hold almost to their imprisoned position.

Many other flowers will dry quite well given ordinary and natural treatment as outlined above, but much depends on the season and the maturity of the blooms when cut. It is always well worth while trying some flowers if you like to have dried flower arrangements about the house during the winter.

A slightly more complex and more expensive method of drying many flowers involves the use of borax or silica gel. These can be bought from most chemist shops and although comparatively expensive it must be realised that they can be used again and again, which drastically reduces their cost per flower. Lay the flowers in the material and sift more very gently over them until the complete flower is covered. One flower must not touch another and the borax or silica must cover intimately every tiny piece of plant material. After an interval of a few days to a few weeks the flower will have dried completely and the borax or silica can then be dried out again ready for re-use. Experiments will indicate which flowers can be dried efficiently by this method, but in general it is probably safe to say that the wetter and fleshier flowers may be the more difficult they will be to dry by this or any other method. On the other hand it is sometimes possible to achieve the most surprising results and the enthusiast will eagerly try all methods with varying maturities of flowers and with the failures will come a surprising degree and range of successes.

Flowers are all very well, but a real flower arrangement evolves only when some foliage is used. Dried foliage is again particularly useful for it can be used not only with dried flowers but with fresh, as a background and a filler which is long lasting and economical. A certain amount of experiment is again called for, because seasons differ and time of collection is critical, but in general many of the tough but smooth leaves such as beech, hawthorn, oak and chestnut can be dried successfully. Begin collecting branches for preserving when the tree is beginning to turn golden before losing its leaves for the winter. When some branches are changing colour choose those that are still green, for this means that they are still capable of absorbing moisture.

Cut your branches, bring them home and stand them in water, preferably warm water, while you prepare your preserving mixture. This should consist of two parts water to one part of industrial glycerine, much cheaper than medicinal. Boil these together very gently and as soon as they reach boiling point pour the solution into a tall can or bucket into which the stem ends of the branches should be stood, the solution reaching about two to three inches up their stems. Leave them there until the leaves have a slightly glossy and silky sheen to them and then remove and use, for they have been preserved. If the foliage fails to take the solution this is quickly apparent, for the leaves merely turn brown, shrivel and begin to drop. In this case remove them from the solution and discard them, for they will never be of any value.

All foliage treated in this way changes colour to a certain extent. Greens turn a light tan or a deep chocolate or leather colour, depending on the maturity of the foliage and the length of time they are left in the solution. The important thing is that they are now preserved and will last indefinitely so long as they are not arranged in water. If they are to be used for a flower arrangement they should always be used out of water and any fresh flowers used with them should be stood in a separate container containing the water they require.

But flowers and foliage are only the beginnings of materials for home decoration which can successfully be dried for winter decoration or for the home which is so warmed by central heating that neither cut flowers nor house plants will live for long. There are many kinds of seed heads, nuts, fruits, cones, grasses, skeletonised materials, barks, lichens and other natural materials which because of their shape, form, colour, texture or gardening connotation render them attractive subjects for indoor decoration with or instead of fresh flowers and plants.

Space does not permit all the necessary details of handling and treatment for the development of all these materials into winter decorative subjects, but the enthusiast will be able to find other and more specialised literature or be able to find by experiment which of the methods of handling is most successful.

Display of helichrysum and barley in a wicker basket

Miniature cotoneaster

9 BONSAI

Bonsai is of Japanese origin and is the art of dwarfing and shaping a young tree to enable it to live for long periods in a miniature and attractive form. Some examples of bonsai are known to be many hundreds of years old, and although young specimens can still have a certain charm, it is the ancient, venerable, twisted and gnarled trees that have greatest appeal. It is possible to buy examples for comparatively small sums and it is also possible to see (though seldom to buy) finer and older specimens for what amounts to a small fortune. On the other hand, it is also possible to find, grow and train your own.

Bonsai trees should not be kept in the home for long periods. Their place is outdoors, preferably in some protected spot where they can enjoy normal outdoor humidity and changes of atmosphere but where exceptional conditions of wet, wind and cold can do them no real harm. If brought indoors they must be kept in a cool, airy spot and returned outside again in a week or so.

Much of the charm of bonsai lies in the containers in which the tiny trees grow and if a specimen is bought it is always preferable that it should be already planted up in an attractive container rather than loose, merely on its own root ball or in a standard flower pot. If you try to grow and develop your own miniature tree choose its container with the greatest care so that container and plant form a pleasing and harmonious whole.

Although containers can, of course, be of any pleasing and fitting shape, most of those from Japan (where the art originated and was brought to its peak of perfection) are low, almost flat and tray-like, which poses certain problems.

The fact that a tree has been bought instead of grown and trained at home does not mean that it will remain in perfect condition without further treatment. As the trees are alive they are bound to grow and the processes of dwarfing and shaping must be carried out continuously during the life of the tree.

Miniature chamaecyparis

These processes are basically only two in number: keeping those portions of the plant below and above soil level short and in good health and forming trunk and branches into pleasing shapes by means of pruning and bending.

Almost any tree can be dwarfed. In fact it is easier and always more successful to use a type that normally would grow to a considerable size than to try to dwarf and train a naturally small tree. Pines and conifers are usually best for the beginner and evergreens generally are best both because they continue attractive in the winter and because it is quickly apparent when something is wrong, whereas a deciduous tree can die during the winter without making this really apparent until next spring.

Any tiny tree can be chosen, but a considerable portion of your task will have been naturally performed for you if you can find one growing in shallow soil, among rocks on a hillside or perhaps even in a pile of debris such as the site of a ruined building. For here roots will be naturally stunted and the growth may very well be equally restricted or even bent and twisted by a stone resting on it. If such a seedling tree is found, take it up carefully, damaging the roots as little as possible, and

Miniature juniper

plant it in a normal flower pot in a good soil mixture with added sand for sharp drainage.

Alternatively it is usually better to grow your own tree from seed as by this means you have control of every part of the young plant right from the beginning. Sow fresh seed in shallow boxes or pans and place in a cold frame or some similar protected spot outdoors. The germination process may take some time, but when the young plants are large enough to handle safely, at least an inch tall, prick them out carefully into small individual pots, compressed peat pots, waxed paper containers or even into a half grapefruit or orange. Keep these individual specimens still in the frame and preferably plunged in moist peat or some similar substance which will ensure that the roots are never allowed to become dry.

As growth appears pinch out any shoots which grow too tall or in the wrong direction. Begin looking critically at the shape of the tiny plant. After a few months lift the plant and look at the root system. Cut out completely any thick and over-strong roots, using a sharp knife, scissors or secateurs and lightly trim the more fibrous and hairy roots. Re-pot as quickly as possible and firm the soil carefully about the roots again.

In the second year growth is likely to be more rapid. Continue the pinching, pruning and training process, and in addition begin to train any branches that in your opinion need to be bent or curved. You can do this by bending the branch very carefully with the fingers and then keeping it in position with a tiny splint, by attaching a small stone to weight it down, by tying it to a toothpick speared into the soil, or best and most professionally, by twining a short piece of soft copper wire around the branch and then bending it into position. Do not attempt too drastic a training all at once. Better to train a young branch a little at a time.

For the first two or three years it may be necessary to root- and branch-prune at least twice a year, in spring and autumn, but when at the end of this time the young tree, by now fairly well shaped and adapted to its small size, appears attractive and settled enough for its permanent container, it can be removed from its nursery bed and planted up. The container should be glazed and have good drainage holes, for apart from appearance and decorative value this makes the general principles of care and culture both easier and safer.

Miniature juniper

Spread the roots carefully and sift soil over them gently but firmly so that every root hair is in close and intimate contact with the soil and no air pockets are left. In some cases it may be helpful to weight down one or two roots with a piece of rock, and if selected with an eye to appearance a rock or two can add to the attraction of the ensemble as a whole.

Watering and feeding must obviously be carried out very carefully. The roots must be kept constantly moist but they must never become waterlogged. Feeding must be sufficient to keep the plant in good health but not such that it spurs the plant into unwanted growth. So in very general terms it might be advised that the young plant receives an egg-cupful of water each day and a very weak dose of liquid fertilizer or a sprinkling of bonemeal once a month during the growing season. A light spray over the foliage on occasions is also helpful.

Training to shape and root and branch pruning will probably only be necessary once a year in the spring by now. Remove the tree very carefully from its container and gently scrape away some of the soil around the roots. Trim the roots, again cutting away completely any new thick and heavy roots that may have developed and merely snipping the tips of the root hairs. Re-plant, adding a little fresh soil to replace that which is exhausted or has been removed.

Never remove too much growth above or below the soil at once, but spread the process over an entire year. If one particularly large branch is to be removed entirely, let this be the complete treatment for a month or so. Trees require leaves for their health and nourishment and if too many are removed at once the young tree will suffer.

Never keep a bonsai specimen indoors during winter. In summer plants can go indoors for a week or so at a time, but in winter the atmosphere is invariably too hot and dry. On the other hand no bonsai specimen should be exposed to the elements completely during winter. Give some light protection against rain, snow and frost. A covered porch or patio is the best place, covering the container and possibly the entire plant with loose straw or even sheets of newspaper pinned into place if the frost is heavy.

Striking display of arums in a tall glass jug

10 FLOWER ARRANGEMENTS FOR EFFECT

All flowers are beautiful. Some are beautiful because of their shape, some because of their colour or combinations of colours. Many, though not all, give us a bonus of perfume. If they are beautiful in themselves it is reasonable to ask why it should be necessary to arrange them for home decoration. Is it not enough merely to enjoy them for themselves?

The answer to this question is twofold: in the first place if flowers are beautiful in themselves it seems only proper that the greatest possible advantage should be taken of their beauty. When we have a fine piece of furniture we place it in the home so that it shows to greatest advantage and we groom it and take care of it. A flower arrangement uses the beauty of the flowers in a pattern, a place or a colour combination related to its surroundings, bringing added beauty to the flowers and the surroundings.

Secondly the arrangement of flowers is the practice of sensible economy. A bunch of flowers brought into the house from the garden or bought from store or market and merely pushed into a pitcher or vase is uneconomic because a considerable proportion of the flowers will be hidden from view. They become a flower mass, a blob of colour. Flower arrangement should reveal every flower in all its glory, should relate each separate flower to its neighbour and should blend the whole into a shape or pattern of significance to its surroundings.

If we are going to arrange flowers into a shape or pattern it follows that we must have some means of holding them in position so that they are secure and maintain their placement. The type of arrangement aid we use will be dictated to some extent by the shape of the flower container we use, but basically there are three different types of flower holders, all efficient when used correctly, which can be used either alone or in combination.

The first, cheapest and most versatile is ordinary large mesh chicken wire. As this is crumpled into a rough

Arrangement of mixed carnations in a silver bowl

ball shape a mesh of $1\frac{1}{2}$ to 2 inches is best and most malleable. This is pushed into the container so that it holds firm and the flower stems are passed through the various openings and held securely.

Cut a piece of wire netting roughly as wide as the container and twice as deep or long. Screw it up and push it into the container cut ends uppermost so that flower stems will be held by it both at top and at base. The wiry ends to the piece which have been left exposed at the top can be most useful, for one or two can be hooked around the top edge of the container to hold the netting firmly in position and it may also be helpful to use others to encircle any particularly difficult or recalcitrant stem.

This method more or less fills the entire container with wire netting, but there may be occasions when only a portion of the container is to be used for flowers, as, for example, when a long low dish is to be used with the flowers placed only at one end. In this case to fill the entire container with wire mesh would be both wasteful and ugly. So in circumstances such as these crumple the netting into a ball large enough to hold the flowers and fix it to the base of the container where you wish your flowers to stand. This can be done quite simply by taking a small ball of ordinary modelling clay and pressing this firmly on to the base of the dry container. The netting pressed into this will be held firmly in place.

Arrangement of chrysanthemums and beech leaves

Another type of flower holder, particularly suitable in the circumstances just outlined, is called a pinholder and it consists of a heavy metal base, usually lead, containing the heads of a number of nails or pins so that the sharp ends project upwards to pierce and hold the flower stems. Pinholders can be bought in several shapes and sizes to suit different purposes. I have said that they are heavy, but they can nevertheless slip about on the floor of a wide container, so again we use modelling clay to hold them in position. In this case the most efficient holder is made by taking three small pills of clay, pressing them firmly to the base of the dry pinholder and then pressing this on to the floor of the container. Both surfaces must be absolutely dry, otherwise the clay will not adhere.

The third type of flower holder consists of two types and formulations of foamed plastic material, both water absorbent, into which stems are pushed and are then held securely. The first is called Florapak, available in white or green blocks about nine inches square and three inches thick. The second type is called Oasis, green only, available both in rectangular blocks again or as circles which fit neatly into the necks of many containers. Neither type is expensive and although not as long lasting as either wire mesh or a pinholder both can be used several times before it is discarded. Yet even after being used several times in flower arrangements both these materials have a future value as a packing material for house plants, where their moisture absorbing qualities are so helpful.

Florapak requires careful and thorough soaking before it is used, for it takes some time to absorb water, but Oasis soaks up water very quickly, which means that the arrangement can be completed in the dry material before adding water.

But now, having chosen the vase or container and the type of flower holder best suited to both container and the shape or pattern of the arrangement you desire, how and where do you begin? The answer to this question will depend, of course, on the arrangement, but for simplicity's sake let us begin with a circular dome or half sphere which is to be placed, shall we say, on the centre of a large table.

A circular bowl will probably be best for this type of arrangement, so this should first be filled with wire mesh as suggested earlier. The first stem to go in position will be exactly in the centre of the bowl. This is the most important stem in the entire arrangement, so it is well to look at it more closely. In the first place this will be the only vertical stem and secondly it will be the tallest, thus setting the height pattern for the arrangement. It should be not less than one and a half times the height of the bowl for the most pleasing proportions, although it can be taller. As it is the only vertical stem, all other flowers should appear to radiate from its base.

So, with the central stem in position setting the overall height limit, now decide how wide the arrangement is to be. Place one stem at right angles to the first on one side and then another of equal length opposite it on the other. This determines the width of the arrangement and the circle should be completed by two more right angled stems at ninety degrees to these. We now have the central vertical flower and coming from its base four radiating stems, and together these five stems show us how large the arrangement will be. To get our circular arrangement all the side stems are of the same length, but if we wish it to be wider or narrower we have only to lengthen or shorten the stems in the right direction and they in turn will set the pattern.

Pelargonium
One of the oldest and most favoured ot ındoor pot plants. Many varieties are now available.

Viburnum
Many of the species provide colourful berries, red, black, blue or yellow, for winter arrangements.

Two arrangements of gladioli. Left exploits the long stems making it a vertical feature and right masses the flower heads, also vertically

8

Having obtained our outline we have only to fill in the spaces between the basic five stems. Bear in mind that the central stem must be the tallest and it must be the only completely vertical stem, so all other stems should have their ends so near the base of the first that they give the impression of radiating from the same point. This, after all, is how plants grow naturally, and although the flower arrangement is artificially contrived the more natural the arrangement then the more attractive it will be.

This type of arrangement is meant to be viewed from any side, so it is called an all round arrangement and it obviously is designed for the centre of a table. But most of our home arrangements will be placed on a table, a sideboard or some other piece of furniture which is against a wall and so will be seen only from the front. Facing front arrangements demand a slightly different technique, for their backs are more or less flat, suitable for being placed flat against a wall.

As with an all round arrangement the first stem to go in position is the tallest and only vertical one, but here, if the arrangement is to be a quarter rather than half circle, this tallest vertical stem goes in the centre of the container but against the back wall and instead of four stems at right angles to it there will be only three to set the limit of the dimensions. Fill in between these primary stems in exactly the same way as before.

This basic technique, in fact, is used for all types and patterns of flower arrangement and having mastered the few and simple rules it is possible to go on to making more complex patterns. To make an L-shaped arrangement, for example, the tallest vertical stem goes in position and is followed by only two stems at right angles, one fairly long going out to the side and the second shorter coming out to the front and the outline is again filled in.

Remember in all flower arrangements to make the artifice appear natural, to conceal the technique. Thus the ugly wire netting, pinholder or plastic flower mount must always be completely invisible in the finished arrangement. It is usually possible to hide the holder by means of flower stems or foliage, but if the style of arrangement will not permit this, then use shells, stone, driftwood or even a single leaf or flower to conceal the fact that the arrangement is held and maintained in position by artificial means. The only real difficulty in doing this is when the container is of glass. If a glass bowl is used the flower stems will usually hide the stem holder, but if the container is tall and slim we must slightly change our technique.

In a tall, slim arrangement, whether in glass or a more opaque container, the stems will be held in position more or less by the walls. So we do not need to have wire netting filling the container but merely in the neck so that we can position our flowers. So screw up the wire mesh to fit in the neck, arrange the stems through this so they go down to the base and are thus anchored. The netting in the neck is now easily hidden by flowers and only the long stems show through the glass, where they take on a new beauty through glass and water.

The basic techniques of flower arrangement are only a means to an end, this being the creation of a work of art, the assembly of flowers and foliage in a design or pattern with a particular purpose in mind and bearing the stamp of the personality of the arranger. But unless the techniques are understood and carried out faithfully no arrangement will succeed, for once having been placed in position the flowers must remain where they have been put. If they move then the design will be spoilt.

So having dealt briefly with the mechanics of arranging flowers we come to the less straightforward and more personal matters of personal taste. The practised and experienced member of a flower club will be able at a glance to determine the authorship of an arrangement because personality is impressed in the design in just the same way that a Dutch old master flower painting differs from one by Matisse or Cezanne. This is largely concerned with the use of colour.

Colour is always a somewhat complex matter, and flower colour is rendered even more complex by the fact that few flowers are of one colour alone. The closer one examines a flower the more one will see in it. For example, beside me as I write are some roses which one would normally call red. Yet in the red are hints of pink, blue, purple, and at the base of the petals here and there a touch of white. Many other flowers are even more complex, with definite rather than hinted secondary or even tertiary colourings. All of these colours will be taken into account by the skilled flower arranger, perhaps the secondary colour being echoed in a second flower and so on.

Red, yellow and blue are primary colours, by which

Arrangement of chrysanthemums, ferns and dried leaves in a pottery vase

we mean that we cannot make them by mixing any other colours, yet the main spectrum colours are these three plus orange (a mixture of red and yellow), green (a mixture of yellow and blue) and violet (a mixture of blue and red). And again, colours are variable, for if we say something is blue it can mean that there is so much black in it that it becomes navy blue, or so much white in it that it becomes sky blue. In the first place we will say that it is a shade of blue and in the second that it is a tint. The various gradations from dark to light are known as tones.

And there are even more complications ahead. All growing things, for example, have some green in them, so whatever flower colour you use you must also consider the ever present green. This green may always be present but it will not always be the same green, but various tints and shades.

Sweet peas, on the other hand, can be red, pink, white, cream, purple and almost black, yet they all merge together and an arrangement made with all these colours can be most beautiful. But do not be lulled into a false sense of security because of this fact. Introduce a marigold or a poppy and you will see at once that the many colourings of the sweet peas merge happily because they are members of the same family and that if a stranger enter the fold discord enters with him.

Arrangement of trumpet lilies, copper beech leaves and horse-chestnut flowers

So we see that botany too must be considered when making our choice of flowers, added to which there are the questions of the colour of the container being used and the colours of the furnishings or surroundings in which the completed flower arrangement is to be placed.

But though I have pointed out the complexities in this question of colour, they are, in fact, simple enough to resolve with a few minutes thought. We all know that the only six colours we really know, red, orange, yellow, green, blue and violet, can be made into a colour wheel, each colour merging gradually into the next. The mere fact that the colours merge naturally gives us a clue to what will appear both natural and pleasing.

If we cut the colour wheel vertically down the centre we have in one section red, orange, yellow and green, all colours which blend well together. In the other section we have green, blue, purple and red, again all colours which blend well together. So neighbouring or analogous colours harmonise.

But an arrangement of nasturtiums, shall we say, set in an orange vase and placed in a room basically decorated in yellow may very well be harmonious and pleasing, but to some tastes and at some times it may be a little insipid. Just as we sometimes need a little spice or seasoning in our food to bring out the true piquancy of flavour, so we sometimes need a touch of contrast to show our flowers at their best.

Once again the colour wheel helps us here, for we see that red is directly opposite green, orange directly opposite blue and yellow opposite violet. These are complementary colours, and we see again that each of the primaries is opposite a secondary.

Now simply because they are complementary to each other, two such colours used together both appear brighter than they do when used alone or separately. So we must use a little discretion in complementary colour harmonies and soften the resulting clash in some way, either by making one of the two colours predominate or by introducing the convenient and ever present buffer colour of green in the form of extra foliage.

But these are all theories and when working too close to them one sometimes comes upon an unanswered question. Few flowers conform exactly to the colour wheel and many do not fit it at all, particularly those known as broken colours, browns, russets, olives, creams and greys. These broken colours predominate in dried flowers and foliage and as they do not conform to the rules we must make up our own as we go along.

This is, in fact, one of the many joys and challenges in the whole diverse art of decorating with flowers and plants: the fact that although there exist a very few basic rules, they are there merely for our guidance. They are our flowers and our plants and we can do with them what we wish. It is possible to break every rule in the book and produce a striking, beautiful decoration for the home and it is even probable that by twisting the rules slightly according to personal tastes and inclinations one will produce an effect which bears the stamp of your own personality, a genuine, creative work of art.

TABLE 1
SELECTIVE PLANTS FOR THE HOUSE

Name	Colour	Height in ft.	Habit of growth	Use
Adiantum	Green	½–2	Small segmented fronds on wiry black stems	With other ferns in cool summer arrangements
Aechmea	Grey-green	1–2	Leaves radiating from central "vase". Long-lasting pink flower	As specimen when in flower, in groups otherwise
Aglaonema	Green with white or other markings	1–2	Large, spear-shaped leaves on long stems	Alone or in big, bold groupings
Anthurium	Green	1½–2½	Glossy leaves and vivid flowers with "piggy tail"	Alone when in full flower, in groups otherwise
Aphelandra	Green, white-banded leaves	¾–2	Cockscomb of vivid orange-yellow flowers	Alone when in full flower, in groups otherwise
Araucaria	Grey-green	½–2	Tree-like	In groups
Aspidistra	Dark green	1–3	Spear-shaped leaves	Singly or in groups
Azalea	Pink, red or white flowers	¾–2	Bushy, with shining green leaves	Large specimens singly, small in groups
Begonia	Various, flowers and foliage	½–1	Varied	Depending on kind
Beloperone	Green, pinkish flowers	½–1½	Bushy	Good specimens singly, otherwise in groups
Calathea	Green with markings	¾–2	Spear-shaped leaves on long upright stems	Good specimens singly, otherwise in groups
Chlorophytum	Green and white	½–2	Grass-like striped leaves in rosette	Singly, placed high to allow plantlets to hang downwards
Chrysanthemum	Various	1–3	Usually bushy, many flowered	Use singly as colour harmony
Cineraria	Various	½–1	As above	As above
Cissus	Green	½–10	Climbing vine	Trained to cover wall or grow up cane

Name	Colour	Height in ft.	Habit of growth	Use
Codiaeum	Various	½–2	Various shaped, coloured and sized leaves. Vivid	Singly as specimen
Coleus	Various	½–2	Bushy, vivid soft leaves in many colours	As above
Columnea	Green	½–3	Trailer with vivid scarlet or orange tubular flowers	As specimen placed high to allow trails to fall
Cordyline	Green and red	1–2	Spear shaped leaves in green, scarlet, mauve	Good specimens singly, otherwise in groups
Cryptanthus	Various	¼–2	Many forms and colours	Usually singly
Cyclamen	Red, white, pink	½–1½	Pretty flowers above pretty, grey-green leaves	Singly or grouped with other cyclamen
Cyperus	Green	½–1½	Umbrella spokes of leaves on upright stems	Singly or in groups
Dieffenbachia	Green and white	1–2½	Large, beautifully marked leaves	Singly
Dizygotheca	Bronze	1–3	Tree-like with long, elegant, serrated leaves	As specimen until leaves begin to drop, then in groups
Dracaena	Green, white-margined	¾–2	Various forms	Good specimens singly, otherwise in groups
Erica	Pink or white	½–1	Bushy heathers	Best as specimens
Euphorbia	Green, scarlet flowers	½–2	Thorned stems, small green leaves, vivid but tiny red flowers	As specimen
Fatshedera	Green or variegated	½–10	Tree-like, usually on tall single stem	Tall specimens singly
Ficus	Green or variegated	1–10	Tree-like with large, glossy, oval leaves	As specimen
Fittonia	Green, silver-veined	½–¾	Beautiful, large, low growing leaves	Specimen
Hedera	Green or variegated	½–10	Climbing ivy, many forms and colours	As screen, wall covering or trained up stake
Helxine	Green	¼	Soil covering, with many tiny leaves	As specimen or in groups

Name	Colour	Height in ft.	Habit of growth	Use
Hyacinth	Various	½–1	Flower spikes	Singly or in groups
Hypocyrta	Green	½	Soil covering, with bright orange-red flowers	Singly or in groups
Impatiens	Various	½–3	Green or bronze forms, with red, orange, brick or white flowers	Singly or in groups
Kalanchoe	Various	½–2	Various forms with fleshy green or coloured leaves and various flowers	Singly or in groups
Maranta	Green, with pink and chocolate	½–1	Beautifully marked foliage	Singly. Good for bottle gardens
Monstera	Green or variegated	1–10	Climbing vine with large, slashed and holed leaves	Specimen or trained up wall or stake
Narcissus	Yellow or white	½–2	Familiar bulb flowers	Specimens or in groups of spring flowers
Neoregelia	Green, white-striped	½–1	Saw-toothed, strap-like leaves growing from central "vase"	Specimen
Nidularium	Green	½–1	as above	as above
Pandanus	Green and gold	1–2	Grass-like, with large striped leaves	Good specimens singly, otherwise grouped
Pelargonium	Various	½–10	Familiar "geranium" with many forms	as above
Peperomia	Green or variegated	½–1	Several forms	In groups
Philodendron	Green	½–10	Climbing vine with heart-shaped leaves	Wall or stake covering
Platycerium	Grey-green	1–2	Fleshy fern with leaves like antlers	Specimen
Plectranthus	Green	½–10	Climber or trailer with shining circular leaves	As specimen with trails climbing or hanging
Primula	Various	½–2	Several forms	Specimen
Rhoicissus	Green	1–10	Climbing vine	Specimen to cover wall or cane

Name	Colour	Height in ft.	Habit of growth	Use
Saintpaulia	Various	½	Furry leaved plant with small violet shaped flowers in several colours	Specimens or in groups with others
Sansevieria	Variegated green	½–3	Long, fleshy, spear-shaped leaves	Specimen or in groups
Saxifraga	Red-green	½	Strawberry-like leaves with long runners bearing baby plants	Specimen, held high to let runners fall
Scindapsus	Variegated green	½–5	Climbing vine	Specimen, grown up cane
Solanum	Scarlet or orange	½–1	Attractive berried Christmas plant	Specimen or in groups
Spathiphyllum	Green	1–2	Green, spear-shaped leaves and white flowers	Specimen or in groups. Good for dark spots
Syngonium	Green	1–2	Goose-foot shaped leaves	In groups
Tetrastigma	Green	1–10	Vigorous climbing vine with chestnut-shaped leaves	Specimen. Will grow 20 ft. in a season
Tradescantia	Various	½–4	Familiar climber and trailer	Good plants as specimens
Vriesia	Green with markings	1	Rosettes of strap-like leaves	Specimens
Zebrina	Various	½–4	Larger, fleshier, more vividly coloured tradescantia	Specimen
Zygocactus	Various	½–2	Crab-claw-like green foliage with many white, pink or red flowers	Specimen or in groups with others

TABLE 2

FLOWERS, FOLIAGE AND FRUITS FOR CUTTING

(Tabulated by season)

AC = autumn colour
B = berries or fruits
V = variegated foliage
G = green or glaucous
DF = decorative foliage
E = evergreen foliage
F = can be cut and forced any time after shortest day

WINTER (Dec., Jan., Feb.)

Shrubs and trees

Garrya elliptica, catkins, E, G
Cornus, coloured stems
Ilex (holly), B, E, V
Chamaecyparis lawsoniana lutea, E
Erica (heather), pink and white
Chaenomeles, pink, orange, red, F
Prunus, in variety, F
Chimonanthus fragrans (wintersweet), yellow, mahogany, F
Daphne mezereum, mauve and D. laureola, green
Eleagnus, E, V
Mahonia, E

Bulbs

Galanthus (snowdrops), white

Herbaceous

Helleborus niger (Christmas rose), white
Iris foetidissima, B
Vinca major variegata, V, F
Lunaria (Honesty), white seed cases
Iris unguicularis, lavender blue

SPRING (March, April, May)

Shrubs and trees

Aralia, deciduous, varied, no blue
Forsythia intermedia spectabilis, yellow, F
Prunus (all types), mainly pink, some white, F
Ribes, rose-red and yellow, F
Magnolia soulangeana, white flushed purple

Rhododendron, many types, all colours
Cytisus, varied, all colours
Syringa (lilac), white, rose, primrose
Camellia, varied, mainly pink, white and red, E
Pieris forrestii, creamy white, brilliant young foliage

Bulbs, corms, tubers

Narcissi, yellow, white, pink
Tulips, all colours except true blue
Freesia hybrida, all colours except true blue
Fritillaria imperialis, orange and yellow

Herbaceous

Euphorbia epithymoides, sulphur yellow
Doronicum plantagineum, yellow
Cheiranthus cheiri (wallflowers), primrose to red
Pyrethrum, pink, rose and purple-red
Trollius, yellow and orange
Paeonies, white, yellow, pink, red
Helleborus corsicus, green
Helleborus orientalis, dusky pink, DF
Bergenia, rosy-pink, DF
Epimedium, lemon-yellow, DF
Lamium galeobdolon variegatum, yellow, DF

SUMMER (June, July, August)

Shrubs and trees

Roses, in variety, species for autumn colour and fruits
Viburnum, white, AC, F
Philadelphus, white
Rhododendron, see Spring
Senecio laxifolius, E, G
Hydrangea, varied, white, blue, rose
Hypericum, B

Bulbs

Iris, blue, yellow, white
Lilium, in variety, white, yellow, pink, orange, red, green
Alstroemeria, orange, pink
Agapanthus, blue

Herbaceous

Geranium, varied, DF
Euphorbia griffithii, orange
Ligularia clivorum, DF
Dianthus, in variety, white, pink, red, mauve
Alchemilla mollis, yellow, DF
Gaillardia, red and yellow

Hosta, V, G, DF
Lathyrus odoratus, (sweet peas), varied
Delphinium, mainly blue, but other colours
Chrysanthemums, varied, no blue
Aquilegia, varied, all colours
Antirrhinum, varied, no blue
Clarkia, varied, no blue
Matthiola (stocks), varied, no blue
Nicotiana, varied, no blue, green

AUTUMN (Sept., Oct., Nov.)

Shrubs and trees

Roses, see Summer
Viburnum, see Summer, AC
Sorbus, in variety, B, AC
Pyracantha, in variety, B
Cotoneaster, in variety, B
Aralia, AC
Fothergilla, AC
Euonymus, B, AC
Symphoricarpos, B
Malus, B

Bulbs

Amaryllis belladonna, magenta
Nerine bowdenii, magenta
Gladiolus, all colours
Acidanthera, white, purple blotch

Herbaceous

Dahlias, in variety, no true blue
Aster (Michaelmas daisies), in variety, no yellow
Chrysanthemum, see Summer
Anemone japonica, white, rose
Tagetes (African marigold), yellow, orange
Kniphofia, varied, white to orange
Physalis franchettii, B

Index